D0059678

Limber

Limber

essays

angela pelster

Sarabande  Books

LOUISVILLE, KENTUCKY

Managing Editor
Sarabande Books, Inc.
2234 Dundee Road, Suite 200
Louisville, KY 40205

Library of Congress Cataloging-in-Publication Data

Pelster, Angela, 1975–
[Essays. Selections]
Limber / Angela Pelster. — First edition.
    pages cm
Summary: "A startling essay collection charting the world's history through holes in the ground, rings across wood, mountains, figs, and a body's evolution. Essays move from her rural Canadian childhood to a desert in Niger, where "The Loneliest Tree in the World" once grew. Deeply thought and wholly original, Limber asks what it means to live on our inherited planet"—Provided by publisher.
Includes bibliographical references and index.
ISBN 978-1-936747-75-7 (pbk.)
I. Title.
PS3616.E44A6 2014
814'.6—dc23

2013031028

Cover design and interior art by Kristen Radtke.

Interior layout by Kirkby Gann Tittle.

Manufactured in Canada.

This book is printed on acid-free paper.

Sarabande Books is a nonprofit literary organization.

This project is supported in part by an award from the National Endowment for the Arts.

The Kentucky Arts Council, the state arts agency, supports Sarabande Books with state tax dollars and federal funding from the National Endowment for the Arts.

for Mom

CONTENTS

Les Oiseaux

It is still winter.

The cedar waxwings swarmed the backyard this afternoon—at least a thousand of them—and the radio I had been listening to went static with their coming and then switched to a French station that I could not understand. I moved from my table to the window to watch the birds feed on the red mountain ash berries. Poor trees. They looked so patient in the snow, so resigned to being stripped of their color for the sake of the birds.

When the waxwings were done, they lifted from the branches as one enormous body and the frequency of my radio pulled out with them and rode on the backs of their wings until the station went static and changed to English again. It all happened smoothly and without fanfare, as if waxwings had always controlled such things in the universe.

I ran to another window to follow them for as long as I could while the announcer rolled through the top of the hourly news: The mutilated remains of a ten-year-old girl have been found in a park today.

It has been discovered that trees communicate with one another below ground through root systems and fungi. I do not know if they communicate with birds, but it seems possible in a world where all manner of unimaginable things happen in places seen and unseen, in forests and gardens and parks.

The trees in the backyard were stoic in the aftermath of the birds, with scraps of red scattered on the snow below them, and the radio droned on. I stood at the window and sent out signals from the top of my head for the birds to return. I tapped the tips of my fingers with my thumbs; we waited.

By Way of Beginning

THIS IS NOT A MEMOIR, but the summer I was nine my parents borrowed a grass-green camper van and loaded up the four of us kids to drive to Disneyland from our home in Alberta. The camper was only meant to accommodate four, so my youngest sister slept in the large cupboard over the driver's cab, peeking out like a cuckoo bird above us in the morning, and my little, skinny-chested brother slept on the floor in the space between the table and the seats in front of it. I shared a bed with my oldest sister. We didn't mind being cramped. We were used to the six of us driving together in my dad's pickup truck, three on the seat and another three piled on top of those. The youngest always on my dad's lap because she was small and didn't get in the way of the steering wheel so much.

6

•

The Trees of Mystery is one of those roadside attractions that pull travel-tired families in from the highway and toss them into strange, dreamlike worlds while they stretch their legs and turn cheap souvenirs over in their hands. It is an almost mile-long trail through a section of redwoods in California, close to the southern border of Oregon and the only stop I remember making with my family on our thirty-hour drive. It was the kind of place with redwoods large enough to drive a van through, and where families of six would try to hold hands around a trunk but couldn't. Everything smelled of rotting plants, of bursting spores and red dirt and moss. Mushrooms, big enough to sit on, bloomed from the sides of trees and the air was so wet you could suck the rain from it with your lips.

We were from the prairies. We were used to wheat and barley rolling for miles under the blue with clumps of poplar trees edging the fields to stop the wind. Poplars are small narrow trees with leaves that clack in the slightest breeze, and I spent my summers building tree forts in them with my cousin who lived down the road. We dragged old bits of lumber and a rusty bucket of nails that my dad had given us into the forest and hammered the first board in as high as we could reach on tiptoe. When we had the rickety floor laid, we climbed up onto it and swayed with the wind, imagining what we would build when we were old enough to use power tools.

The poplars fed the tent caterpillars that infested our land year after year, and I came to think of summer as the season of the caterpillar and the poplar tree as a nest for their spontaneous reproduction. Every summer, until the county started to spray the forests with pesticides from planes, the pale bark of our trees squirmed with black mounds a foot long and two inches deep of tent caterpillars. They dropped from the branches and landed in our hair, on the backs of our necks, in our collars. My older sister squished them with her bike on the concrete and recorded the color of their guts in a coiled book; my brother froze them under a spurting propane tank and snapped them in half; my little sister put one on her tongue to feel the furriness of it tickle before she swallowed it down. I remember looking out the bedroom window one morning and seeing that our bright green summer had been eaten into an early winter. It was such a mean-hearted thing to do to a place on the constant edge of freezing. When I saw the redwoods at the Trees of Mystery, I never wanted to see a poplar again.

There was a forty-nine-foot-tall statue of Paul Bunyan at the gates, along with his thirty-five-foot-tall Babe the Blue Ox. The signs scattered around the grounds said that Paul could bring down twenty-five million feet of wood a day. When he was born, it took five storks to carry him. He ate fifty eggs at breakfast and ten sacks of potatoes; his parents kept ten cows to supply him with milk for the day. The signs also said that the tallest tree in the world is a redwood in California. It was the land of giants, I thought, and difficult to know where the myth began and the truth ended. Ask a poplar if it believes in redwoods and it might start talking about faith.

At the head of the trail was a slice of smoothed and varnished tree that hung like a target with arrows pointing to rings of important dates. I touched my finger to the year the Magna Carta was signed, the year Columbus set sail, the year Canada became a country, the year Paul Bunyan was born. Tree, tree, tree; there was always tree.

A tree ring marks a year of growth, but it isn't marking it for humans. The rings are a memory of what the seasons brought and what the tree made of it. The widest rings are the good years, recorded in thick dark circles of brown, and the hungry years are narrow and pale and hard to read.

A German artist named Bartholomäus Traubeck sliced a slab of tree as thin and round as a record and placed it on a turntable. The rings were read as data that told the years of strength and growth rate and climate and rainfall. They were mapped to scale and translated by a program that reads the information and outputs it as piano music. So the turntable turns with a record of wood, and its years are given a voice that sounds like my cloudy-eyed grandmother at her upright, stumbling, trying to remember the sad songs she liked to play when she was young. It is full of longing. I am not surprised. The wood that is being played is dead. It is a map of the memory of a year following a year following a year, a selective story of what happened and sometimes of what it meant.

Once, there was a year without summer, and it was so cold that it snowed in June and nothing bloomed and no fruit grew, and the trees didn't record that year in their rings; there is a missing line. But when the tree's life is placed on the record player there is no pause to mark this, just a skipping on to the next year, which is to say that even a tree will only tell the story it wants to tell.

Burmis

A SINGLE DROP OF MELTING ICE water on the top of Snow Dome in the Canadian Rocky Mountains has three end-point oceans to choose from—the Pacific, the Arctic or the Atlantic. One slide down a mountain face and the water droplet turns nomadic, wandering thousands of miles from home, carrying bits of granite wherever it goes. The Continental Divide runs through the Rocky Mountains and splits the province of Alberta from British Columbia, but the Crowsnest Pass, that has served as a route through the Rockies for thousands of years, stitches them back together again.

The Burmis Tree is a local landmark that stands alone on a small rise by the side of the highway through the Pass. It is slightly famous among nature photographers for the way its knotted arms reach out to the mountains and the moody mountain skies.

It is a limber pine. Limber pines are named for the ways they bend in the harsh winds and grow in curves around it; they slither their roots along rock faces until they find cracks they can slip into and drink from. Under prime conditions, they can reach heights of twenty-meters-tall, though in Alberta, they usually only make it to three meters. They look like twisted saplings because of the stony ground and the wind and winter stunting their growth, but they can live for centuries. The sprouting Burmis Tree anchored itself to a block of sandstone centuries ago, and grew as it could along the highway when the highway came along. But now the Tree is stripped of its bark, and the wind has cleaned it smooth as a piece of driftwood and the sun has bleached it white. All year round it stands as naked as a skeleton in the shadow of Turtle Mountain.

The Burmis Tree is named after the mining town of Burmis, Alberta. It was one of nearly a dozen small towns that sprang up when coal was discovered in the Pass and a railway blasted through the mountains. "You just had to get used to the bumps," the wives of the miners used to say when Turtle Mountain shimmied and the ground moved beneath their feet. "Maybe the dishes would rattle in the house, or the pictures would fall off the wall." The women learned to shrug, to pick the frames up and slug another nail into the wood while their men scraped coal from the mines like a coyote cleaning a carcass.

Ten thousand years before the Burmis Tree sprouted, the Clovis and Cordilleran people lived in the Pass and mined for chert in waist-deep pits to remove the flint-like rock for their knives and spears and arrowheads. They left traces of their living in scooped-out hollows of ground facing Turtle Mountain. After them, the Agate Basin people moved in like new tenants, and then the Mummy Cave culture in 4000 BCE and the Pelican Lake culture in 1000 BCE. The valleys teemed with herds of elk and deer and bison, and the rivers frothed pink with salmon. Even in years of drought the mountains snagged the clouds and pulled the rain to the earth and the people came, kept coming, following the trails of food into the heart of the mountains.

In 1500 BCE, the Ktunaxa and the Piikani settled their lives into the land and smoothed tepee rings into the flats, shaped sacred sites for spear and hoop games and placed stones in sleeping circles. They hunted and fought in the valley with weapons made of the mountains they had mined for generations, for centuries, until the 1730s. Then the people broke out in pink spots, they started to bleed, their heads pounded like fire drums, their backs grew weak and their arms were as frail as the grandfathers. The spots turned to scabs on the infected bodies by the eighth day, but by the eighth day, the bodies were mostly dead. And then the lush mountain valley became a bowl of rotting flesh, and the people who escaped the pox stayed away from the Pass and the darkness that it held. After ten thousand years, the Pass was emptied of its human inhabitants.

When the white man discovered coal in the mountains they swarmed over the peaks like ants on fermenting fruit, despite the warnings from the remaining Ktunaxa who watched from a distance. It was not just the sickness, they said, it was that the mountain had absorbed their sorrow. "Once," they said, telling the new tenant an old story to explain, "the Cree and the Blackfoot fought here. And while they made war the mountain shook in anger at the brothers killing brothers. A boulder broke from the side of it and fell, crushing the warriors, killing two hundred of them." The Ktunaxa, they told the white men, understood that this meant to stay away. They named it the Mountain That Walked because it moved a little every year.

But the new settler who wanted the mountain called it Turtle Mountain, because it looked like a turtle. He built a town in its shadow and sunk a mine into its guts. He called the town Frank, after himself.

The town of Frank, said Frank, was going to be the Pittsburgh of Western Canada. The mountain peaks were divided into coal and not coal and bit into with axes and dynamite. Within one year there were streets in Frank with hotels and grocers, saloons, a photographer, a school, churches and a cold sulfur spring for health. The valley was filled with miners from Great Britain, America, Ukraine, Russia, Poland, Italy, Hungary, Scandinavia, Belgium, France, and the Balkans. They were men who had been working underground since they were twelve years old, and they were men who had never set foot in a mine before. They did not share a common language; they were strangers and strange to one another.

Eventually, women followed their husbands into their new lives. They birthed and raised their children in tiny cottages on the outskirts of town, hardly big enough for two but often housing ten, and they rehung pictures on the walls whenever the mountain shook. They shoved fear down into their stomachs like medicine, like the tablespoons of vegetable compound that the traveling salesman sold them at their doors for "woman problems." If the women had hoped for more than what they found in the valley, they kept it to themselves, or buried it beneath the soil with the seeds that sprouted spindly and yellow; if the men had hoped for more, they dug harder into the mountain.

There are tours now down the road from the Burmis Tree in the closed Bellevue mine where all light dissolves into tarry darkness a short distance from the entrance. A stream of water rushes past on the left, dripping rocks glow rust red and orange and yellow in the light of the headlamps, and calcified emergency phones from different eras line the walls like museum displays. There is a seam of coal three thousand feet large here, but there is so much of it that the mine doesn't go down but across. Tunnels follow the coal vein for so many horizontal kilometers that it could take a man an hour and a half to walk in the solid black to his underground work. The freezing wind that blows through the shaft on the tour is damp and smells of clay. "A miner earned fifty cents for every ton of coal pulled from the mountain in 1907. Ask any miner now," says the guide, "and he'd jump at the chance to mine again. They loved it."

I've toured mines before. No one has ever said they loved them. There are red-brown smears of blood over the entrances to the mines in Bolivia from animal sacrifices made to appease the devil, and the mines sweat like the men toiling inside them, dropping minerals like oozing wounds onto miners' heads and shoulders and hands. At the heart of every Bolivian mine is a Tio—a man-sized statue with teeth of glass, long ears, and a violently erect penis. The men bring him offerings of coca leaves, bottles of alcohol, and piles of coins in the hope of surviving the hungry earth. They say that above ground they are Christians, but when they go below they enter the devil's world. The life expectancy for a Bolivian miner is thirty-five years.

A Canadian mine is not a Bolivian mine, I am told. And the miners in the Crowsnest Pass dealt with their ever-present threat of death by taking out their lunches at the start of a shift and eating one half of their sandwiches together. Sometimes they sang:

When you're just about fagged, and you've sure lost your
　　punch
What joy to relax while you have a wee lunch.
You joke with the rest and you laugh while you dine
With your battered old piece-can down deep in the mine.

"It was a sacred time for them," the guide said. "A miner knew he might need the man who was eating beside him to dig him out if the methane gas ignited or the mine bumped.

At the end of the shift, the miners stood in a line and washed each other's backs. The man at the front came round to get the man at the end when his was done. There was a great sense of community."

There is a mass grave for miners down the road from the Burmis Tree, just off the highway. It is full of men in their early twenties and thirties lying beneath messy grasses and crumbling headstones. The low fence that surrounds their plot is rusting, and scraggly pines drop needles like blankets over the mounds. There is a tall marble memorial to the Hillcrest mining disaster. A single explosion snuffed out one hundred eighty-nine men from a town of 1000. Pictures of that day show families gathered and waiting on the hills after the emergency whistle blew over their rooftops. The women wear long white dresses and pretty hats, with their children sitting beside them. At first, it looks as though they are out for a picnic after church, but they are leaning against filthy coal cars, sitting in ditches beside the railway tracks, in patches of bare dirt, in shock, waiting for their husbands' bodies to be pulled from the rubble and matched up with their missing parts by volunteers. But who knows a husband's hands like his wife?

Those who escaped with their hands returned to mining, many within the month. They coughed black blood into basins at night and they mined; coal prices fell and they mined; family beckoned from elsewhere and they mined; sons fastened headlamps to foreheads and followed them into the dark, and still they mined. For twenty-six years the Crowsnest

Pass hummed like a hive full of bees and the miners' cottages shook and the wives slung hammers and the men hauled coal. Rocks and lives burst into flame every few months below ground and four hundred fifty-one men died. A few families threw their clothes into bags and fled after each disaster, but most stayed. The men had grown used to the dark, the way it held them, floated them like water, pinched closed the bright edges of worried wives and multiplying children, the boredom of high noon and the irritation of daylight. The dark focused their vision on the one thing, the smooth black coal stamped with curling fronds of fern or ancient maple leaves, or shells like enormous snails, and even once a fish as big as a man's palm, scales pressed into the coal like pottery designs. They shoveled it all into mine cars, hauled it through the tunnels, dumped it into the tipples, ate their sandwiches together, and collected their pay. They weren't afraid to leave; they stayed because they wanted it.

They wanted the mountain the way a lover can want the flesh, blindly, without knowledge or care of the consequence. And so one night, droplets of melted snow water collected on the top of Turtle Mountain and slipped over eroding sandstone, under layers of shale, and nestled into limestone cracks that traveled deep into the face of the mountain. The temperature fell, and crystals of ice bloomed in the pooled water, pushing out against the rock that held it. The mountain strained against the swelling, but its strength had been hollowed by the miners. The ice grew, limestone popped, fissures sped through the stone, and the mountain gave way with a thunderous crack.

Ninety million tons of rock broke away from the face and dropped. The falling rock created a sucking wind. It inhaled the mud of the river bottom with a gulp and spit a wave of violence before it. A miner, a man, a husband and father of seven, sat below the mountain, outside the mine, eating a sandwich on his break. It picked him up and tossed him into the roiling rocks, dancing, all muscle and softness among their sharp mineral, traveling for meters through the air until gravity grabbed him back.

The wave of mud rushed to the town of Frank and divided it into safe and not safe. It drowned the blacksmith shop, railway cars, the power plant, the livery stable, the construction camp, the cemetery, the shoe store, the dairy farm, the bunkhouse, the farmhouse. The boulders slammed against each other and sparked; the charged air shot lightning. The wives and children who slept in the miners' cottages woke once to the crack of breaking mountain, to blink and start in the dark before the mud wall was upon them, throwing houses off foundations, snapping legs and arms and small wrists, cheekbones and backs and necks. Like a glass under a faucet, in ninety seconds flat, the valley, the river, the outskirts of Frank were filled to the brim with rock thirty meters deep.

.

In over a hundred years since the slide, little has grown back. The river changed course, but the rocks that cover the valley for three square kilometers look as though they have just fallen there, the dust just settled. In a paradise of pine green it is a desert of stone, though a small copse of trees has taken over the part of town that the slide ground through. Frank had a population of six hundred then; nearly one hundred died in the slide, left buried wherever the wave deposited them. The survivors on the safe side of town continued to live alongside the dead, as if their neighbors and their neighbors' houses beneath the limestone existed in a secret other world, as if they still hung bed sheets to dry on the clotheslines below ground, swept floors, cooked dinner in the dark. The mine was up and running again within months, never at a loss for workers, though Frank, the man and the founder and the owner of the mine, lost his mind sometime later.

The town of Burmis is gone now. The only trace of it left is a plaque where the schoolhouse once stood. It died when an oil geyser shot up through a barley field on the Alberta prairies and the Canadian Pacific Railroad switched from coal to electric. All the mines in the Pass died then and most of the towns too. Frank survives because of its dead, but just barely. A multi-million-dollar interpretive center is perched on the rubble of the slide, facing Turtle Mountain. The center is a popular tourist stop along the almost deserted Pass, but it is unclear as to what it is interpreting. After fifty years since the mines have closed, there are still old miners who dream of those black days and the heft of that shining rock in their hands. Geologists say it is only a matter of time before the mountain moves again.

Even the Burmis Tree is dead. It died of heart rot in its heartwood. Heartwood is what grows at the center of a tree. It is created from a spontaneous chemical transformation which can't be controlled or predicted, and which could as easily be called magic. It turns the heartwood dark, protects it from rot, and then, when the process is complete, kills it. Magician and murderer at once.

But *dead* doesn't matter to a tree as much as *rotten* does. Sapwood is the outer layer of wood on a trunk beneath the bark and around the heartwood. It stays alive when the heartwood has died, and carries water to the leaves and roots and hoards it away in times of drought.

But every deep wound, broken branch, fire scar, sliced root, and boring bug invites the fungus that causes heart rot to enter. The fungus grows, softening and weakening the wood, making it vulnerable to strong winds and breaking. It is a wonder that as many trees manage to avoid rot as do. A tree can live for generations when its heart has rotted out. The Burmis was over six hundred years old when it died.

The Burmis Tree stood by the side of the highway for twenty years after its death, anchored to the rock by the roots that once fed it. But on a cold autumn night, while the forest of pines moaned and it bent in the fierce wind, the brittle tree broke under the strain and fell to the ground. In the morning, the people that still lived in the Pass gathered around the fallen pieces. Eventually, someone fetched a chain and another brought a truck. They drilled a rod into the Burmis Tree's trunk and another into the ground; they wound chains around its limbs and clamped steel over its roots; then they hoisted it upright and bolted it back to its position of splendor against Turtle Mountain.

There is a moment in every mine tour when the guide has taken the visitors as far as they are allowed, and then stops and turns. There is no light leaking in from the entrance, no bulbs overhead, no electronics of any kind blinking green in the dark, just headlamps flashing against the insides of a mountain. "On the count of three," the guide says, "I want everyone to switch off their lamps."

"One,

"Two,

"Three."

There is some fumbling and nervous giggling, but they are all eventually turned off. Pupils fly wide open to suck in any remaining light, but there is nothing for them to grab. Silence settles in with the black. It becomes difficult to ignore the weight of the earth pressing in from above and the rumbling of the devil below. Even old mines are pitch black and full of death, and desire holds hands with despair in them—any soft city tourist can sense the wrestling, not only in the stories of the dead and injured, but in the survivors' unyielding need to stay despite the death and injury. Melting ice on the top of a mountain has more choices before it. There is no difference to whether or not you stand in the dark of a mine with your eyes opened or closed, except for the one of having tried to look and found nothing. When the lamps are switched back on again everything is the same.

There is a pullout on the side of the road, and a sign that says the Burmis Tree is a symbol of endurance for the people of the Pass. But the Burmis Tree is dead, and death is as far from endurance as is possible. Hope beyond reason leads to death, it seems, as does despair, as does reasonable hope, but any way there is eventually a release. Not even a tree can stay strung to the side of a mountain forever.

A few years ago, some vandals sawed off one of the Burmis Tree's naked white arms, but the locals picked it up and glued it back onto its trunk. It seems that the possibility of leaving it on the ground never even occurred to them.

Ethan Lockwood

DURING THE COLDEST WINTERS in the province of Alberta, when the temperature drops to -40, boys bring out their mini hockey sticks to Christmas parties and take shots on net in their coach's empty basement. Upstairs, their parents will stand with drinks in one hand and crackers scooping up hot artichoke dip in the other, while a few women will put casserole dishes in the oven to reheat. There will be a pile of cards on the counter from every player thanking the coach for his time, a gift card from Tim Horton's Donuts tucked inside them all. Each boy will have stood at the front door with his hair combed nicely and with a buttoned-up cotton shirt beneath his coat, and have shyly handed an envelope to the coach, mumbling his thanks before running down to the basement with his stick.

But one December, it was warmer than anyone remembered, warmer than snow, warmer than all the records, warm enough to make the doomsday sayers say that God had left and the world was melting to hell. It would be a green Christmas, other people said, as if things had turned tropical. But that was a strange name for it, because everything green had died to brown, and the brown wanted the snow to make it beautiful. So the boys brought their real sticks, ducked their shy hellos at the door, and dragged the net out from the basement and onto the road.

They hardly even needed their coats. They pulled their toques off their heads and threw them to the sidewalk, divvied up the players, and someone dropped a puck for the faceoff. The backs of their necks were sweaty within minutes and their party clothes wrinkled and damp against their skinny chests. They played hard like they did on the ice, but for fun, switching sides and fighting, jabbing ribs, swearing and giggling. They took cheap shots and turns in net. When the sun began to set and the temperature dropped, they felt the cold settle between their spines and lungs, and their mouths turned to little smokestacks spewing white air over the suburban yards. Someone's dad had already hollered at them once to put their coats back on. Dinner would be ready in five minutes. Time to come inside.

The boys thought of plates of food and warmth and the game on the TV in the basement while their parents ate upstairs, and they felt the emptiness of their stomachs all at once. But there was still time for just another shot, and then maybe another. Two of the boys scuffled with their sticks, and Ethan Lockwood, who had turned to go inside because it had been his father calling, saw the last chance for a good shot and hurried toward the puck that was rolling free. He ran to his friends, caught his stick in theirs, caught his feet in his own ten-year-old feet, and tripped. He fell into a bush edging the neighbor's yard.

A branch in the bush entered Ethan's right eye. It traveled through his eyeball, through the socket, past his skull, and punctured his brain. There was no snow to catch the blood or his body, only brown grass and dirt.

Miraculously, the doctors said, it did not kill him. Miraculously, he was only paralyzed on the left side of his body, admitted to intensive care while his brain swelled and fought off infection. millimeter to the left or right would have ended everything, they said. He is a lucky boy, they said.

A Google search of Ethan Lockwood reveals another boy in another city wearing a too-large T-shirt that reads, "You make your own luck."

I have been writing letters. They are along the lines of "Dear Sir/Madam, I know that this is strange and that I am a stranger to you, but could you please tell me what kind of bush hurt Ethan." I want the name of the plant so that I might search until I come to the evil heart of it. Somewhere, I know I can find a story of the bad luck this wood brings—of its use in witches' spells three hundred years ago, or of the way it can be tucked into an enemy's satchel to bring illness or heartache or loss of money. There will be something, some bit of long-forgotten knowledge that we have lost on our scientifically proven way to explain it all. But no one has written back yet.

So I wonder at his name instead. Lockwood. I wonder if he has thought of how it predicted this event, if he hates his name now, if he wants a new one like Brown or Smith, if he wonders why he was the one to have fallen, or if he is proud that he locked fates with wood and came out the victor. Doctors say he is determined to walk again. He will play hockey again, he says.

For seven years my last name was not my own but the one I took from a man I loved once. If I do not love him anymore, is his name and the implication of it still mine? What leaves should I twist in my hair to keep safe? What prayers should I write out and roll into scrolls to tie around my neck? I do not believe in a cruel God. Earth is tilted on its axis just so; a degree to the left or right and we would be no more. Perhaps this is evidence of intelligent design and possibly evidence of tenderness. It is difficult to know how to read the signs, which things to be thankful for, how to love this place.

Meditations on a Tree Frog

FROGS HAVE TEETH on the roofs of their mouths.

Frogs do not drink, but absorb water through their skin.

A group of frogs is called an army.

Frogs close their eyes when they eat and press them into their heads to force food down their throats.

There are tree frogs living in the maple across the street. I sit on the porch with my friends and tip my chair onto its back legs for hours. We eat chocolate bars and popcorn like we are watching a movie of the people passing, and we drink until late, until the cicadas stop their chain-sawing and the birds tuck their beaks under their wingpits and the ripping croaks begin.

"What is that noise?" I ask one night, because tree frogs are absurdly loud for the one-and-a-half inches of space they consume. "I don't know," they all say. One friend suggests frogs. "Do we even have tree frogs in Iowa?" I ask, but no one knows. And so I check. And we do—grey tree frogs that change color to match what they're sitting on, from white to black to gray or green, though when they are dead they go gray. They are singing to find a mate. I read some more.

The scientific word for "frog" comes from the Greek, *anura*, meaning "without tail." However, frogs used to be called *salientia* from the Latin, *salere*, "to jump," and the English word *frog* comes from the Proto-Germanic meaning "hopper," which makes me wonder how it was decided that the jump was the trait to name this animal after and not the croak. Or why the taillessness and not the bulgy-eyed-ness. And when did we stop understanding that we named things for what they do, and how did we forget so much? Language sprouts legs like a tadpole and morphs meanings without a trace of the old in the new. We say "frog" and think we are saying a name instead of a description.

I want to know what else we have forgotten. The word "man" is from the Old English *mann*, and this, I think, is disappointing. I had been hoping for "penis" or "hairiness" or "sex-ing," though what does catch my attention is that *mann* was originally a gender-neutral term. Once, in the English language, *mann* really did mean all of us. But before Old English there was Proto-Germanic, and before that Proto-Indo-European, and in ways that I do not understand but accept like a child accepts that the Earth is round though it looks anything but, some linguists say that the word *mann* is connected to the meaning "to think" and that Latin borrows it for "mental," "mind," and "remember."

If a frog is a "to jump" and we are a "to think," then maybe at the heart of *mann* is a brain and not a heart at all. We have not named ourselves "to love," though we do and guide our lives by it. Scientists say that at best we can hold onto feeling in love for seven years. That the seven-year itch is really a matter of chemicals, that a brain can only stay drunk on love for a short period of time until it cries out for rest. Because no matter how we begin, one day you will turn to me and hate my crooked front teeth that you once found endearingly imperfect, and I will look at you and find boring your stories that had once seemed so profound. It is inevitable. But at the center of a word is the thing we have forgotten and the thing it really is, and at the arrival of an exhausted love is the "to think" itself.

A frog jumps, a *mann* thinks, and in thinking is the thing she is. This essay is a love song. In seventy times seven years I will not love you at all. Then, I will think you until all thinking burns off, until what is left of me is a heart in a maple croaking all night long.

The Boys of Lake Karachay

WHEN THE FISH IN LAKE KARACHAY, south of the Ural Mountains in Russia, went blind, not everyone stopped eating them. It was only a game. The boys, bored on a hot summer day, would wander down to the lake through the forest and pull off shirts and pants and splash into the murkiness, jump on one other's backs and spit lake water into the air from their sunburnt lips. It was always warmer in Karachay than any other lake. When they had cooled off, they stood with their toes shoved into the silty bottom, knees bent, eyes flicking over the surface, hands hovering. The fish came to nibble at their calves and ankles, and even blind they could turn and flick away from the boys' diving hands as fast as light winking off glass, as if turned by some secret code.

The fish had milky-blue eyes that bulged and reminded the boys of the old Red Army soldiers that sometimes wandered into the village and sat with tin cups and crusts of salt dried around their lids and lashes, stunned and hungry. The fishes' gills opened and closed in panicky gasps and seized in the boys' hands until the boys knocked them on the head. They filleted them and roasted them over a small fire, plucking the hot white meat from the sticks.

Once, one of the boys caught a fish and yelled at the others to come see. They splashed toward him where he stood with his catch held far from his skinny white chest. It was a small carp, slick and silver-brown with fat gray lips and both of its eyes on one side of its head. The boys laughed and poked at it, brought it back to the shore and sliced it open on a hot rock in the sun. They dug around in its guts looking for other oddities, and then dared each other to eat chunks of it raw. One boy picked up the head and flung it at the back of another with a bloody thunk.

Sometimes after they had eaten, the boys climbed the limbs of the old fir trees. At first, they called out to one other, threw twigs and cones and laughed as they rocked, hands sticky with sap, but as the sun dropped their voices did too, and they went silent as the last birds called from their nests, a forest of boys swaying in the twilight. Their fathers had done this before them. And their fathers, too. Later, they dropped to the ground and went home stinking of fish and lake grass, to mothers who scolded them and scrubbed their backs and arms and faces in water so hot it turned their soft skin pink.

When the restriction notices went up in town about drinking water from the Techa River or eating the fish in it or in the lakes nearby, everyone obeyed at first. Forty miles of dark foam floated on the surface like a frothy plague of water turned to blood. Trucks left the nearby Mayak chemical plant and traveled the road like a conveyor belt to the shores of the river. They dumped load after load into it and then even more into Lake Karachay. There were rumors of a poison reaching the Atlantic.

One day, men came and dammed the Techa River, and then, after years of thin living and war and empty chairs like gravestones at the dinner table, there was a rich riverbed that had once been under water. Everyone who could grabbed a piece and planted it. People started drinking the water again, and there was a feast of fish though the fish were blind.

Gardens were sown and harvested and sown and harvested, and the boys, nearly men, saw Rusalka in their dreams. She swam through the waters of Lake Karachay, her tail silver-green as she rode the small waves like sea foam, and was carried to the shore where the boys watched, tied in silence. When her tail touched sand, it split, formed feet and legs and she walked from the water toward them, smooth and naked as a pearl. The boys followed her to the edge of the beach where the fir trees met the shore. She climbed and perched in the arms of the branches, singing songs that made their breathing turn to clacking as they climbed the tree after her, and their mothers in the shape of flopping fish on the rocks called out to go no nearer. And then at once they were in the water drowning, Rusalka's silver hair in their mouths, her tail around their legs, pulling them deeper.

The boys woke drenched and panting, gums swollen, blood smeared over their white teeth the night of the explosion. The Mayak plant was burning. A two-and-a-half-meter-thick concrete lid shot into the air and landed thirty meters away. Dissolved nuclear waste rose in smoke, collected like a cloud, and shadowed the land five miles wide as it rained over the province of Chelyabinsk. It rained on the houses, the thatched roofs, the gardens of carrots and potatoes and leeks; it rained on the cattle, the sheep, the pigs lolling in the cool mud; it rained on the forest of fir and pine along the rivers, on the meadow grasses of the steppes, the clover and the caragana shrubs, on the badgers and the polecats and the bears digging for bugs in the damp under rocks. And it blew in the open windows, settled on the baked bread, on the jugs of milk, and on the boys eating at the table, drinking from tin cups.

Then the fish weren't blind, they were dead. And the boys weren't boys anymore, they looked like old men, aching and brittle, faces red and splotchy, vomiting and weak. Skin sloughed off their cheeks and foreheads and hands in large sheets, while their mothers eyed them at dinner with growing terror and the food that none of them could now eat.

The towns along the Techa River were gathered up like fruit, first one, and then months later another, and then another. The army came and notices were posted again, and the people were collected and carried away from their homes. Their houses were burned and the top layer of their land scraped from the earth, gray scabs of rock where nothing grew again, the wild animals as homeless as the people, the trees and flowers and grasses, homeless. Dead fir trees in the dead ground. And none of the villagers were told why.

They went to the hospitals—the boys and mothers and sisters and fathers all nauseated and weak and sweating in the night. Rusalka called to them all from Karachay. There was a bead of sweat on the doctor's upper lip when he called it *blood disease* and *vegetative syndrome*, but no one knew what vegetative syndrome was, so the people called it river sickness. The doctor could do little to help, so the people went home again. The mothers boiled broth and said prayers in the four corners of each room, the fathers flipped through old seed catalogs, and the sisters chose names for babies that would never be born.

The boys died panicked and confused in homes not their own, tugging at the blankets knit by their mothers. Lake Karachay continued to shrink while trucks from the Mayak plant, patched and producing again, slipped their loads into the dark water. The dusty banks of the old lake absorbed the secrets they planted in it, and it contracted deeper and deeper into itself, until it was a wet shadow on the dry land.

One night, maybe the townsfolk say, the ghosts of the boys climbed the dead fir trees along the shore and called to Rusalka until she came up from the lake, wailing, in coarse black hair, eyes growing on her hands and neck, her feet webbed and her breasts gaping wounds. As she rose, her wailing grew louder and the dead boys moaned with her, cracking the dome of imposed silence that sealed Chelyabinsk. She started to spin, slowly at first and then gathering speed, flying like a cyclone over the dried lakebed, gathering up the poisoned dust like a spinning spool with thread, she moved to the center of Karachay, rose high above the trees, a screeching storm, until she finally burst, and all the throbbing dust released into the winds that carried it out to the villages for miles around. The fir trees shook in its wake, leaves and needles and seeds sucked into the rush, and the ghost boys felt their ghostly skin prick at the evil passing of it.

The Karachay dust blew its way over four hundred thousand people, while men in white coveralls came to the lake and filled the bed with concrete blocks to pin the poison down. But the land had already revolted and would not be contained. A lake turned weapon—the concentrations so lethal that a single hour standing on its shores changed any living thing into a ghost. And people turned afraid, as the land turned against them.

In 2009, Artyom Sidorkin had trouble breathing. He was a boy-faced man with red hair and a soft voice—when he spoke, he lowered his eyes. He lived in the Ural Mountains, four hundred kilometers away from the Mayak chemical plant, and he did not want to go down to the city of Izhevsk and the hospital there. He hated the city, but he was coughing up blood. It was like needles in his chest when he inhaled, and no one wondered what this meant.

In the Udmurtian Cancer Center, Dr. Kamashev showed Artyom the scan of his lungs. The doctor traced the outline of the tumor with the tip of his ballpoint pen. It was so large that even he, this man from the mountains, could tell where it was. "I've seen hundreds of these before," Kamashev said, "and it must be removed at once." Artyom nodded; he was twenty-eight years old, and he was going to die.

Even cancer cells only want to live; life will take hold of life wherever it can. What the surgeon would say later is that when he made the incision and prepared to remove the tumor, he stopped and blinked three times before calling someone else to come see. What Artyom Sidorkin would say is that nobody knows anything; no one understands how this could have happened. When the surgeon opened Artyom's ribs and cut into his lungs, he found nestled in the red folds and poking into the capillaries a small, green fir tree.

Temple

I'VE READ THAT THERE IS A proper way to eat a fig. You're supposed to take it by the stump, quarter it, then pop the sections into your mouth whole. Delicately. What you're not supposed to do is take it in hand, squeeze it and split it at the seam, because then it's difficult not to notice when it opens red and bursting and wet that it looks like a vulva. Some people are uncomfortable with eating vulvas in public, and so they quarter them instead. But no one is really fooled. Figs look so much like vulvas that the slang for vulva in Italian is fig. And in popular Latin. And Greek.

There are wild figs growing all over the tiny island of Cyprus that floats below Turkey and to the southeast of Greece. A friend who lived there once told me that the trees are two thousand years old—that they sprouted in the same years that the

Holy Spirit flamed in tongues and told the apostle Paul to catch a boat to the island and go evangelizing there. The story goes that Paul liked figs so much that he planted a trail of trees behind him from what was left when he was done eating, and the saplings popped up from the ground like a line of green converts.

I know the apostle Paul. I grew up going to a church that sat on a tall hill between the city and the country and that preached Paul from the pulpit nearly every Sunday. I loved church, even as a kid; I stayed upstairs to listen to the sermons instead of going down to Sunday school with its stupid paper crafts and songs we had to sing in a too-high key. It seems like a miracle now, but all I remember learning in church was that God loved me and that God loved everyone the same. It took me a while, though, to wonder why none of the people telling me about this love from the pulpit had a vulva of their own.

Paul wrote thirteen of the twenty-seven books in the New Testament. He said that our bodies are a temple for the Holy Spirit, and that we should honor God with them. Less beautiful are some of the other sentiments credited to him:

A woman should learn in quietness and full submission.

And

I do not permit a woman to teach a man.

And

Wives, submit yourselves to your own husbands as you do to the Lord. For the husband is the head of the wife. . . .

Paul never married. He said it was better to be single, unless you couldn't control yourself, and then he said, Let them marry: for it is better to marry than to burn.

I went to a Bible college that my church sponsored the year after I graduated high school because I wanted to learn about theology and the mystics and how to shape my life around love. But it was a place where the girls read books on how to picture themselves as spiritually male so that they could be "sons of God" and sometimes, we were asked to stay after class while the wives of visiting teachers taught us about how important it was to allow men to be the "heads of our households" and how fulfilling it was for them to submit to this kind of arrangement. And though I knew enough to argue with them, I did not know enough to not worry that I was wrong.

The unmarried principal with flappy lips and a belly bigger than her breasts threw Paul at us like a firefighter hosing down hell. "Marriage is good, but single is better," she'd quote, then press her lips together and widen her eyes as if we were now all in on the secret. But we were torches. Burning together between the library stacks when she went home and the lights went out. All those Bible concordances watching on with greedy eyes, moans pressed between their pages like dried flowers.

When the apostle Paul was wandering Cyprus, it was during the time when the worship of classical Greek and Roman gods was in full swing, including forced temple prostitution to the goddess of sex. Besides figs and Paul, Cyprus is credited as the birthplace of Aphrodite. Uranus' genitals were sliced off, thrown into the sea, and the goddess of sex and love and beauty rose up from the foam on the beaches. It was Aphrodite's home long before it was Paul's. So when I heard about Paul's figs on Cyprus, I imagined him walking the dirt roads and standing on the beaches, spreading the good news of the love of God and the need for purity, while Aphrodite laughed at his sticky mouth, sweetened from all those vulvas.

But apparently not everyone thought it was funny. Paul preached out against temple prostitution and was tied to a marble column and given forty lashes for preaching there. Some tourists travel to Cyprus just to see that column.

I saw a lot of wild fig trees the summer I spent in Greece, though it wasn't the season for fruit. They were strangler figs, which means the seeds germinate when they are dropped into a crevice of a host tree. As the fig grows, it sends down long, vinelike roots that prop up the stem and eventually bind together to form something that looks like a trunk. It grows around the host and sucks out all its nutrients and steals the sun and rain for itself, until the host dies from starvation. Eventually, all that remains is a tree-shaped hollow in the center of the fig's trunk.

What I know about fig trees is that Moreton Bay figs are the most beautiful of them all. Their roots are so enormous that you can stand between them and lean your head against their curves. They snake out from the trunk onto the ground like a fluid thing frozen, or like a woman's dress pulled into peeks around her while she sits in the grass. They are decidedly feminine.

When I first discovered Moreton Bay figs I wanted them to be Paul's figs, as if he left a string of daughters behind in his puritanical wake. And that maybe they wept for him when he left them and the island. And that maybe they were afraid. Maybe some of them died. Or some of them made a life of waiting for his return. Some of them sat around all day getting fat and watching TV or some of them starved themselves to grow thin, but both did it for the revenge of not knowing what else to do. And maybe some of them eventually stopped waiting, skipped out on temple duty and hopped a ferry. Lived abroad, drank tequila, wrote dirty stories. Maybe the Moreton Figs stopped moving, got jobs, families, raised money for literacy, and then, finally, returned to their old island with gnarled knuckles and tales of giant sequoias and the scent of pine in the winter, their ghost spaces still hollow after all those years.

But I don't know what kind of fig Paul ate, I don't know what grows on Cyprus, so I asked my friend if he remembered. Tell me again about Paul and the figs and those vulvas that he ate and then threw to the ground, I say to him one day.

Figs? He says. They weren't figs, they were olives.

And it occurs to me then how much I still resent the apostle Paul, and how much I want to shame this very dead man for all the centuries of shit he brought women with his writings. And what the hell, I wonder, do I do with olives instead of figs?

•

So Paul the apostle loved olives. He traveled Cyprus preaching the love of God and eating olives. But olive trees belong to Athena, patron goddess of Athens, known for her virginity, and the goddess of war. She earned Athens in a contest with Poseidon by offering the city a better gift than he did. She smacked the ground with her spear and an olive tree sprouted; Poseidon smacked the ground and a spring of saltwater gushed. The people chose the olive because who needs more saltwater when you have the Mediterranean? Her tree is said to stand at the Acropolis still, and the Greeks say that every Greek olive tree can be traced to a cutting from that one.

Olives are the oldest of all fruit trees, and they've been cultivated in the Mediterranean since at least 500 BCE, but have been pickled in salty brine and pressed for oil since 3500 BCE. It was an olive branch that Noah's dove brought back to the ark, olive twigs that decorated the heads of Olympic victors, olive oil that Homer called liquid gold, olive groves that Jesus wept beneath before his crucifixion. He said that a tree is known by its fruit. And that tree, daughter, is an olive.

The olive trees I saw in Greece had hard, smooth berries hanging in the branches, not yet ripe for the picking or the shaking down onto the tarps spread beneath them. The apostle Paul must have known these trees too, or their great grandparents at least. Perhaps, after he had preached in Athens at the Areopagus he wandered over to the Acropolis and saw

Athena's tree. But what does a virgin goddess of war have to say to a man like Paul? Maybe they could have chatted about how great virginity is. Or maybe he reached into her leafy folds with itchy fingers and plucked her ripe fruit. Or at least wanted to.

They could have talked about sexual purity at Athena's tree, and maybe talking about sex would have almost been a substitute for sex, like it sometimes was in the Bible college, and they would have become hot and lusty and intimate without nudity or sin or guilt, and maybe they would have grown tender and vulnerable, as sometimes happens after sex, substitute or not, and maybe they would have unfolded those dark places they kept hidden and also talked regret. And war. And violence. Paul could have told her about his past, and of how he had learned to want nothing more than to put an end to this new cult that had sprung up around Jesus; how he had approved and stood watching as other Pharisees had hurled rocks at a follower named Stephen; how Stephen's face had glowed until it was battered and his nose pushed to the side, how his last words had been the same as Christ's. And Athena could have laid her pretty fingers on Paul's dusty arm, tenderly, virginally, and chosen which of her murders she would tell him about, landing on the worst, the one where she had lost her temper and killed her childhood friend. How she had been so grief-stricken that she made a wooden statue of her and wrapped her in the aegis and set it up on Olympus. And Paul would have felt compelled to say that there was only one true God, but that he understood regret and sorrow, that you don't always grow older and wiser, but sometimes just older and sadder. Athena's warrior shoulders would have softened, Paul's stiff upper lip relaxed, and they would have sat in the shade of the olive together, sex having done what it does best.

I only stayed a single night in the city of Athens and missed Athena's sacred tree. I was on my way through to Istanbul with a friend, and after dinner, we lay on the beach in the dark with Cassiopeia, Orion, Cepheus and the great Cloud of Witnesses looking down from their night sky. Later, we walked back to only one bed in a room for the two of us who had never shared a bed and hadn't planned on doing so. I made a joke of it with his face beside me on the pillow—that I would tell everyone at home we had slept together. He smiled, we lay still under the sheets for years, and then we did. Paul and Athena frowning down on us from their pockets of heaven.

Had Paul visited Athens at the right time, he could have witnessed Athena's feast of Arrhephoria. Two young girls were chosen to live on the Acropolis for a year and tend Athena's olive tree while they wove a new robe for the goddess. At the end of their year, they were given a secret package by one of Athena's priestesses, which they carried on their heads to a sacred underground room. Neither the priestesses nor the girls knew what the package contained, and when they arrived at the room, they left it there and brought back another secret one. Scholars today aren't exactly sure what this feast meant, but they know the name Arrhephoria comes from two Greek words meaning "mystery" and "I carry."

I like to imagine that the packages were empty. And that the girls had sometimes been curious enough to remove the wrappings and found only air inside. As if they could have known that all girls for all years had carried a space that was made sacred by their presence around it.

Paul was uncharacteristically gentle in Athena's city. It was there he said that God is not far from anyone—close enough to be found by everyone. Named among his followers in Athens are women, at a time when women were rarely noticed, let alone named and recorded. It was his third journey by then and perhaps he had learned some things as he traveled. He would be arrested soon after, and the path to his execution by Rome set with no chance for turning back.

There is debate about whether or not the apostle Paul really wrote the book of the Bible named Second Timothy, but if he did, some of his last words were, "Pursue righteousness, faith, love and peace." He said that in God we are all equal—male and female, we are all the same in Christ. He talked a lot about love near the end. I guess we probably all will.

They closed down the Bible college a year after I left, and most of us married in our early twenties, tired of all the burning and before we had learned we could live differently. Some of us lost our faith, some of us became insufferable evangelists, many of us are ashamed of the things we used to believe. Years after we left the college, getting together with friends we had made there seemed like group therapy sessions, like recovering from a trauma. We laughed together nervously and wondered what had happened to us that year. How we could have been drawn into such small and sad ways of living. How sometimes the old guilt came creeping back despite the decision to turn from it.

A friend recently accused me of cherry-picking my faith. She doesn't like the way I throw away the theology I don't agree with anymore and yet still profess belief. I guess I do cherry-pick. It seems like the most responsible way to live out a faith. I'm still only interested in hearing about love.

In Bible college, we were told that everyone had a space inside of them that could only be filled by Jesus. They called it the God-shaped hole, as if we were all strangler figs and had taken root in the divine and sucked the nutrients out of it, until we had sent down such limbs and strength as to stand on our own and were left with the ghost shape of where God once lived. It was an odd way of seeing, I thought, even then. As if God couldn't also be the emptiness itself.

Portrait of a Mango

Mango

Now let us consider the mango tree, for it is rich in food and pleasing to the eye. Its shining evergreen leaves are long and gracious; it provides shade from the sharp-toothed sun to all who seek refuge beneath it. The mango's fruit is sweet in the mouth and calms the nervous stomach; it is a protector of health, rich in phytochemicals and polyphenols, high in fiber and vitamins A, C, and B6. It gives chutney and pickles, salads and syrups, jelly, jam, wine, panha, curries, and lassi. It is dried in strips. It is mixed with condensed milk and used as a topping for shaved ice. It is picked from the tree and eaten raw!

Mango

Indian Yellow is a mystery. Some believe that the Persians invented the pigment and introduced it into India in the late six-teenth century, Dutch painters were using it in the seventeenth;

by the nineteenth century, wrapped boxes of it were arriving in England from India, but no European knew what the yellow color was made of.

The pigment smells like ammonia. Perhaps that's where the story began, and with the letter that was sent by Mr. Mukharji of Calcutta to the Society of Arts in London in 1883, stating that Indian Yellow was made in the small town of Monghyr, India, from the urine of cows fed only mango leaves and water. It is said that they released on command when the urinary organs were slightly stimulated with a hand, something like milking a cow. The urine was collected in buckets, reduced, filtered, and pressed into dirty yellow balls that were washed by European importers. But the cows were malnourished and died young, and when reports of their abuse circulated in England, pressure was put on the government to ban the making of Indian Yellow from mango-leaf piss. The law was passed in the 1890's and Indian Yellow pigment faded from trade and memory, and then from the watercolor paintings that had used it. But not from the oil colors. When mixed with oil and sealed in varnish, the pigment radiates for centuries like the flesh of a freshly sliced mango.

Mango

Though mangoes come in a variety of shapes and are colored from purple to yellow to green to red, only yellow mangoes with a red blush around the shoulders are reserved for North American markets. Red skin is considered a necessity. Though the quality of fruit is inferior, they are more visually pleasing.

Mango

Johannes Vermeer used Indian Yellow pigment in his paintings. It arrived in sealed little boxes that contained the rancid balls of pressed powder the size of a walnut. He mixed them with his oils and voilà! There was the yellow bodice of *The Milkmaid,* the curtain in *The Woman Holding a Balance,* the steeple lit with sunlight in *The View of Delft.*

He was a slow painter, finishing only two paintings a year, using lavish amounts of the most expensive pigments despite his poverty, his wife, his fourteen children. The paintings glow, as if lit from a burning source inside them. What Vermeer understood was light and color, was the way a red dress was never only red, but smoldering blue inside its shadowed folds; the way a wall was pockmarked with light, with every color in the room layered beneath it. He had observed this trick of the eye, that all objects absorb the color of those things nearest it, that nothing is ever seen in the purity of its own pigmentation. Even objects lie, tell stories, are subjective, pretend to be something they are not. It is difficult to know when looking at something beautiful where the beauty is actually coming from.

Mango

We are starving. I've waited too long to stop working and start dinner, and now it is late and there is nothing to cook and school in the morning, and so I say to my daughter who is doing her math homework by herself at the table, "Let's just get in the car and go out for dinner."

But we are so hungry that she is getting grouchy and I'm getting impatient. "If you could have a tree," I say to distract us while I drive, "that grew anything at all, what would it be?"

"Pizza!" she says.

"Steak!" I say.

"Candy," she says.

"Wine," I say.

"Mac and cheese," she says.

"Money!" I say.

"Boring," she says. "Popsicles!"

And then I wake to how winter it is: the gray slush of the roads, the broken grasses in the ditch, deserted sidewalks, my softening body beneath my winter coat, living off pasta and bread and last season's apples, my daughter's pale face in the rearview mirror. All my hunger turns its appetite to summer, and to wonder how I have let us live so far from it.

"Mangoes!" I say.

Mango

Mangoes are the fruit of paradise, and though they are rich in all good things, it should be remembered that they, like a beautiful but fearsome tiger, must be handled carefully. When harvesting mangoes it is important to use caution. The sap that drips from the fruit or oozes from the snapped stem is caustic. If it comes in contact with human flesh, it can cause dermatitis, rashes, and blistering that may require medical attention. If the sap touches its own mango skin, it will leave dark, sunken and unsightly blemishes that will decrease its value at market.

Mango

"Mom," I say to my mother one day. "I just put you in one of my essays."

"Oh?" she says back.

"Yeah. I'm writing about mangoes, and I said something about Vermeer and how much you like the color yellow."

"Oh? Yellow is my favorite color."

"I wrote you into a conversation we haven't had yet. But it could totally happen."

"Alright."

"So can we talk about Vermeer now?"

Mango

Once, in the Buddha's incarnation as King Mahajanaka, he was traveling through a park in the high-noon heat. The sun bit at the back of his neck and pressed heavily against his face, while the heat from the elephant beneath him drenched his legs in sweat. He remembered the white-topped peaks of the Himalayas that he had visited once as a boy, and longed to bury his face in the snow to relieve the terrible burden of the sun. He passed below a monkey perched in the arms of a mango tree, lifting the golden fruit to its mouth and biting away at the juicy flesh. The tree dripped with mangoes, and though the king longed to stop and eat, his retinue hurried him on to the business of the day. So the king decided to return to the tree and eat his fill that night.

The chirruping of the night insects nestled in the undergrowth soothed the king as he walked to the grove carrying his own torch. But when he arrived at the mango tree and held the light high in the darkness, he saw that someone else had been to it before him. It was stripped bare, the branches broken, the leaves scattered. It looked as though it might not live another season. Another full green mango tree stood beside the stripped one. It had not been harmed because it bore no fruit. King Mahajanaka went home to his palace deep in thought. In the morning, he renounced his title and belongings for the troubles they brought to this life.

He would become a tree without fruit. He needed no other teacher.

Mango

Fifteen. Vermeer had fifteen children, not fourteen.

Mango

There is no mention of Jesus eating mangoes in the Bible.

Mango

Nutritional Facts	
Serving Size 1 cup, sliced 165g (165g)	
Amount Per Serving	
Calories 107	Calories from Fat 4
	% Daily Value
Total Fat 0g	
Saturated Fat 0g	1%
Trans Fat	1%
Cholesterol 0mg	0%
Sodium 3mg	0%
Total Carbohydrate 28g	9%
Dietary Fiber 3g	12%
Sugars 24g	
Protein 1g	
Vitamin A	25%*
Vitamin C	76%
Calcium	2%*
Iron	1%

Mango

Mangifera indica

- Ground mango seeds with fresh water can be fed to children discovered in gardens with muddy mouths from eating soil. This will cure them of their desire for earth.

- Women with relaxed walls from too many children should apply a teaspoon of the paste of mango seed inside the vagina half an hour before the husband arrives, and it will bring a virgin feeling.

- Drinking mango juice regularly in the evening eliminates physical weakness.

- Taking half a cup sweet mango juice with 25 grams curd and itsp and ginger juice, 2 or 3 times a day controls loose emotions.

- Taking 10 grams, finely ground powder of mango leaves (dried in shade) with water (kept in a glass tumbler overnight) daily helps in breaking the kidney stones and throwing them out.

- The mango is rightly called the "King of Fruits" for no other fruit is so well-loved and sacred to the people. Praise the King of Fruits. It is also a contraceptive.

Mango

There is a mango on the desk beside me, holding open a book on the history of pigments. I pick up the fruit and smell it often. There is the slightest scent of sweet. Mangoes belong to the highly poisonous plant family Anacardiaceae, and so I know I shouldn't bite into it through the peel, though I want to. My lips already feel a little swollen, a little itchy from all the pressing of it up to my face. I am exhausted by the beauty of its blushing red shoulders. Some days at the grocers, the stacks of yellow bananas next to the Granny Smith apples next to the pink dragon fruit next to the heaped tangerines next to these mangoes fills me with such delight that I think the word "delightful." "Delightful fruit." "Delightful color." "Delightful world." What is this place where food grows on trees like gift-wrapped presents strung on a branch? How could this be? How could I ever be unhappy with these colors in piles around me?

Mango

My mom's favorite color is yellow. I tell her that this is because she is Dutch, because Vermeer loved yellow so much and Vermeer is Holland, so it's in her blood. She can't even help it. All her favorite clothes are yellow, the walls of her house, the pictures on them. I tell her about Vermeer and his expensive pigments and the mango-leaf cow piss.

But no one knows anymore if the mango-leaf cow piss story is true, though it doesn't stop people from telling it. There are no traces left of Indian Yellow pigment-makers in Monghyr, India; there are no records of laws banning mango-leaf fed cows, no remains of the ammonia or nitrogen from urine found in the old balls of yellow powder. There is just the original letter from Mr. Mukharji of Calcutta, the fact that Indian Yellow suddenly disappeared from the market and Vermeer's paintings quietly glowing through the centuries.

Mango

Vermeer died three hundred years to the day before I was born, I tell my mom. "That's interesting," she says.

"Yeah," I say.

In fact, my birthday is December fifteenth which is really just an estimate of the day Vermeer died on since the records mark the day of his funeral and not his death.

I suppose none of it really comes to anything, but I pay attention anyway. I collect the signs like a doctor tapping on a patient's body, looking into ears, pressing on a spine, drawing blood from the unseen places. It is difficult to know when one of these will come to something, when some bit of evidence will be made luminous in the beautiful light, when the world will bend and let slide a little secret from its corner.

Saskatoons

1. Michael walks upstairs from the basement and into the damp heat of the living room. He flops onto the couch like a boneless slab of meat and lies there as if paralyzed. The basement is cooler than this, but it smells like cum. And shit. A pile of shit covered in cum. David shit beside the toilet again, and the staff haven't found it yet. Or maybe they have and don't want to deal with it. David will whine about having to pick it up. And then he'll get mad. "Fucking bitch," he'll say, and the staff will add a swear chore to the cleaning up the shit chore, and he'll raise his soft pale hands and swipe at the air, wanting to swipe at a face, his plump boy boobs jiggling under his T-shirt. Michael wonders what it would be like to take those in his mouth, if they'd feel like a girl's or like pouches of pudding. Probably like pudding. Is he a fag? Does wanting to suck David's boy titties make him a fag?

2. The fan flips the air around but doesn't make it any cooler. One of the staff walks into the kitchen and opens the fridge. She takes out ground beef, dripping a trail of blood on the floor to the stove, and drops it into a frying pan. In a minute, the smell rides on the hot air, dark and moist like old mushrooms. David follows the smell up the stairs from the basement and shuffles into the kitchen to stand at the side of the staff.

"What's for dinner?"

"Tacos."

"Make a lot."

"Yeah. You need to change your shirt before you eat."

"No. Why?"

"There are boogers all over it."

"So."

"It's gross. I don't want to eat looking at your bloody boogers."

"Fuck you."

"You can't eat until you change your shirt. And you can add a swear chore to your regular chores after dinner."

"Stupid bitch," David says, and goes down stairs to change his shirt.

3. When Michael was six, his foster mom made him eat Spring Breeze scented laundry soap for swearing. Spoonfuls of it burning his stomach until he threw it up all over his shoes,

sudsy and fresh. She had stood there with the box of soap and smacked at his head with the metal soup spoon for messing his shoes. She was wearing a bright red shirt; he should have known better. The red shirt or the blue one with the bows on it meant she had woken up with a violence in her. She would squint at him like he was a stranger when he asked her something, or she would keep her head down and swing her hand against his face without looking.

He started paying closer attention after he noticed her shirts. It didn't take long before he could tell just by the sounds of her coming down the stairs what she would be wearing, how she would feel, what she would do when he asked her to sign the field trip permission note from school. He thought it meant he had special mind-reading powers. Like a gift to make up for the other things. When someone noticed his bruises and he was sent to another foster home, it was like his eyes had been plucked from his head or his ears cut off. He couldn't read minds at all.

4. Someone new starts every three or four months at the group home. Once, a woman came and stayed only a few weeks. She was fat and loud with huge tits and wore shirts that stretched thin over her belly rolls. She made fun of the other workers when they weren't around. She told Michael about her boyfriend, what he did to her with ropes once. He could tell she was saying these things because she wanted him to like

her. "You don't need to fight with me like the other staff," she'd say. "Just tell me what you want. I'm reasonable." So he asked to see his case report, had said it all cool and casual like, as if he had seen it before, as if he hadn't been wanting for years to look at its pages, and she had given it to him, pretending she didn't know she wasn't supposed to.

5. It was thinner than he had imagined it would be—a half-filled, three-inch binder with doctors' reports, court orders, and school assessments hole-punched into it. His name written in black Sharpie marker on the spine. The first page was his intake report:

Circle one

- Head lice: y/n
- Sexually active: y/n
- Sexually abused: y/n
- A listing of clothes brought with him:
- T-shirts: 2
- Jeans: 1
- Socks: 3
- Underwear: 3
- Sweaters: 0
- Winter coat: 0
- Boots: 0
- Shoes: 1 pair (too small)
- A tally of bruises, scars, wounds.

The psychiatric assessments: violent tendencies, ADHD, fetal alcohol, below-average intelligence. No one had taken him away from his mother. She had given him up. No other family had wanted him.

Most of the pages were copies of copies, the handwriting a ghost spider skittering off the page. It was good that he saw them now, before it was too late to read them at all. David hadn't wanted to see his. "My mother is a bitch who used to tie me to the toilet," he said. "I'll kill her if I ever see her again." There is a note written on the white board in the staff office that says David is not to take calls from his mother. His mother has never called.

6. Michael saw his mom yesterday. Sometimes she phones after having not talked to him for months, and his pits start sweating as soon as he picks up the phone. He forces himself to speak slowly though she giggles and teases. "Hey, Mikey," she'll say. "I miss you. Want to come stay for a few days? Get away from those whores?" And then they'll both laugh and he'll forget to keep his words slow.

7. Last Christmas, Michael's mom asked him to come for two weeks. He hadn't lived with her for that long since she'd gotten rid of him. He didn't want the staff to help him pack. He knew they'd say he didn't need to take every single thing, but he'd shoved it all in the bag anyway,

sides bulging, zipper gaping open. When he carried it up the stairs, the worker on shift just looked at the bag and raised her eyebrows. It was Christmas holidays. No one wanted to fight about anything. When he was dropped off at his mom's, the staff handed him a plastic garbage bag full of wrapped presents they had bought for him with his "Celebrations" fund from the government. "Merry Christmas," she'd said, and hugged him before she left.

8. His mom put on lipstick and did her hair his second night at her house. "There's a Christmas party downtown," she said. "I'll be back in a bit." But she wasn't. She'd left Michael's baby sister with him, and for a while he did all right. But when the macaroni and the crackers and the cereal and all the frozen ends of bread shoved into the back of the freezer were gone and there was no money to buy anything and his sister wouldn't stop crying and he hadn't remembered to take any of his meds and he was so fucking tired, he cried into the cushions on the couch until the blood vessels burst at the corners of his eyes, and then he called the group home. He yelled at the staff, said he needed a ride back. His hockey duffle was still half-packed; it only took him a minute. Someone came for the baby. The bag full of presents went back to the car, to the group home, spread under the tree there. All the other boys had been sent out to spend the holidays with some family. Michael unwrapped the presents

Christmas morning by himself. The staff who had been called in last minute sat in the kitchen texting on her phone.

9. Yesterday, when his mom had called, she had asked him if he wanted to come over for the afternoon. "I got lasagna," she said. "You can stay for dinner." Michael's pits were sweating. "Yeah, I guess," he said.

They ate on the couch watching The Price Is Right and scraping burnt noodles off the bottom of the tin. "Stouffer's is better," his mom had said during the commercials. "I should of got Stouffer's."

"It's good," he said. "I like it."

"What do they feed you there?" she asked, not turning from the TV.

"I don't know. Spaghetti and chili and stuff."

"They make you eat vegetables?"

"Yeah, but I hate it."

"You eat your fucking vegetables." But she wasn't angry, she was putting on her motherhood like putting on a coat. "It's better than those other places you were."

"Yeah."

"Remember that woman who gave you instant porridge for every meal? And macaroni for a treat?"

"I hate that shit."

"Bitch had it right. No cleaning. No cooking. Just making money off of you." Bob Barker was on the TV again, but his mom kept talking. "That must piss you off. You think about that stuff and get pissed off?"

"I don't know. Maybe."

"Maybe? You just take that shitty food from them and you don't care?"

"I got good stuff now."

She turned and looked at him, looked at his plate scraped clean and smiled, pleased. "Yeah, you do."

10. He went to the museum with his grade six class once, to learn about the shit white people did to the Indians. "Is that your mom?" they asked him at the tepee display. There was a red mannequin with black braids, a deerskin dress, and a baby strapped to her back. She held a wooden bowl full of wrinkled saskatoon berries that she was grinding for pemmican. "Look, it's Michael camping with his mom," one of the girls giggled. "It can't be," Michael said loudly, sweating. "She isn't drunk." Everyone laughed until the teacher shushed them.

They washed their hands in a line at the sink in another room, and mixed flour and shortening and currents in a bowl for bannock. It was lunchtime and the class was hungry. When the pans of bread were pulled from the oven hot and puffy, every hand shot out for a taste. "This is so great," one of his friends said with his mouth full. "I'm not even kidding. You should bring this for lunch every day." Michael nodded back. He had never tasted bannock before. It was good. He hadn't expected to like it. He folded up a copy of the recipe and put it in his pocket.

11. When the staff picked him up from eating lasagna at his mom's house, it was dark but still warm. His mom had fallen asleep on the couch when the lasagna was gone, and he didn't want to wake her, so he left without saying goodbye. They drove home in silence, he was so tired. He stood in the basement outside his bedroom, and the staff told him to hurry up and brush his teeth before bed. "Don't be such a fucking whore," he yelled at her, without wanting to, hardly thinking about it. She moved back slightly, and then gave him a swear chore, turned and climbed the stairs away from him in her ugly dress. He came up behind her then, reached out his hand, and hit her on the calf with the back of his fingers. Smack. Hard enough to sting but not to bruise. She had stopped and stiffened, and Michael felt a hot rush of blood through his throat and into his chest. She turned and looked at him and her eyes were already wet. Her neck flushed. She opened her mouth and closed it.

12. A little bird, he thought.

13. "You bastard," she said.

14. She was new and she was going to cry. She walked up the stairs without saying anything else, into the office and shut the door.

15. He was grounded for the week. The Incident would be recorded on his chart, hole-punched, and placed in his case book, now one page thicker. He had told her he was sorry later, and he had meant it. He liked her good enough. She had nodded back at him after his apology. "It's all right," she had said. "I'm sorry I called you a bastard."

    "Maybe you should get a swear chore, too."

    "This entire job is a swear chore," she said back, and went into the office to write the report.

16. He wonders if she is afraid of being alone with him now. The others were going to a movie after dinner and she was staying behind to supervise him. Once, he heard the staff talking about some woman who was killed at a home. She had been working alone and one of the kids had beaten in her face with a bat. He can imagine it happening. Two years ago, when girls used to live at the home with them, one of them had grabbed a butcher's knife from the dish-

washer and chased the staff around the house with it, screaming that she was going to push it into their eyes. The staff yelled at the boys to go into lockdown and then they barricaded themselves in the office until the cops came.

He's way stronger than her. He can tell from her skinny arms. She can hardly carry all the plates to the table at once. And she only comes up to his chest.

17. "What do you want to do?" she asks, when the dishes are clean and the house is empty except for them.

"I don't know."

"The saskatoons are ripe in the backyard. Want to pick some with me?"

He's never picked berries before. He doesn't really want to.

"Come on. They're so good and it's hot in here."

18. The only thing she can find for a bucket is a plastic box that used to hold mail. She rinses it out and they put on their shoes and go around the house to the back. The ground is soft and spongy around the trees because of the sump pump drainage, and the grass a brighter shade of green than the rest of the yard. He bounces a little in his runners. "Look at them," she says, and pulls a cluster of berries into

her hand. "They fall right off." She has long dark hair in a braid down her back.

19. The mosquitoes are thick by the saskatoon trees, and the repellent makes Michael's lips tingle when he licks his fingers from the first berries he tries. "This is like camping with my mom," he says to her. He tells her all about their summers in the woods, about the hikes they take, about the time they even stayed in one of those tepee campsites.

    "We fried bannock over the fire and I picked some berries to go with it. I can hardly wait until we go this summer."

    He tells her about his baby sister, about how much he loves her, how smart she is—she's already talking and she's only a year old—and about his uncles and aunts and how they always come over to visit when he goes to his mom's and how he wishes he was old enough to live on his own, do what he wants, see his mom all the time. It's the heat. The sweet berries. The soft ground. It's her smiling nicely, nodding and staying quiet. It's that she's new and doesn't know anything. It's the thickness of the air, the sun caught in the trees. Like little pieces of foil hung in the branches. He opens his mouth and all the stories fall out.

20. Michael's box is half full of berries by the time he's done. He stopped picking awhile back and has been holding the high

branches down low for her to reach. They will go inside soon. She'll mix flour and shortening and teach him to roll out a crust. They'll put in sugar with the berries and dot the filling with pats of butter. She'll show him how to pinch the edges of the pie closed with his finger and thumb, and then he'll take a knife and slash his initials across the face of it, sprinkling it with sugar again. When the pie is done baking, he will hold it while she takes his picture, while he tries to look tough in oven mitts. She will stay three years and imagine she loves these boys. She will leave them one month before Michael runs away to live with his uncle, and then to run away from his uncle, to nowhere, disappearing into the cracks of the city forever.

All names are changed to protect the innocent.

The guilty are protected accidentally, since guilt and innocence have not yet been determined.

Inheritance

WILLIAM HENRY JACKSON OF Athens, Georgia, loved a white oak tree. It grows at the corner of Dearing and South Finley still, though William Henry Jackson is long dead. The Tree is marked by a small chain fence, two marble plaques, and a bronze plate which clearly states that this tree is The Tree That Owns Itself, and that the Tree was legally deeded to itself by William Henry Jackson in 1832. It is simple to find and its story engraved for the ages in bronze and stone around it.

Besides the bronze plaque with the date, there are two marble slabs that quote from the original deed. One of the stones is very old with a missing corner and fading script, but both mark the Tree and set it apart from all others: For and in consideration of the great love I bear this tree and the great desire I have for its protection for all time, I convey entire possession of itself and all land within eight feet of the tree on all sides.

So, William Henry Jackson loved the Tree. In 1832 he loved it. Or sometime in the 1830s. Or maybe the 1820s. It is problematic that the original deed has been lost, or we'd know the exact date of when this was written and when William Henry Jackson loved the white oak. The bronze plaque that states the date of the Tree's emancipation was placed there in 1988 and there is conflicting evidence of when the original event actually took place. It seems that someone in 1988 chose a date from the possible dates and engraved one on a plaque and screwed it to the concrete berm around the Tree. As previously mentioned, you can see it all still on the corner of Dearing and South Finley in the city of Athens in Georgia. It has become a bit of a tourist attraction and a small monument to love.

It might also be stated, for the record, that there is some debate about whether or not William Henry Jackson owned the land that the Tree grew on. William Henry Jackson owned the plot of land across from the tree—in those days named Lot #14 and now called #226 Dearing Street. There are papers to prove this. But the tree grew on Lot #15 and nothing has been found to show that Jackson actually, at one point, owned the land that he handed over to the Tree. This practice of taking things that aren't yours and then granting them back to the rightful owner might be explained by the fact that Jackson's father was James Jackson, the Governor of Georgia, who owned slaves and fought fiercely against the abolitionists. The Jacksons must have been in the habit of believing things belonged to them that did not. But then again, it might not explain anything. There are no indications now of what William Henry thought of slavery. Sometimes the apple falls far from the tree, sometimes it does not.

Eventually, the white oak came to be called The Tree That Owns Itself by the locals of Athens, and it was said by them that William Henry Jackson loved the Tree because of the memory of days spent playing under its branches as a boy. It is interesting to note, in the name of verifiable facts, that Jackson didn't grow up in Athens, but in Jefferson County. He moved to Athens, across the street from the Tree, as an adult, so it is unclear now why he loved the Tree as he did. Of course, William Henry died and the Tree lived on and continued to own itself for reasons now lost to us.

The original deed, as mentioned above, is also lost. And there are some who call into question its existence to begin with. The first mention of the deed in print is a front page report from the Athens Banner, dated Tuesday morning, August 12th, 1890. It stated that William Henry Jackson had come to love the Tree as he watched it grow from his childhood. Of course, by that time, William Henry was long dead and unable to correct the records in regards to his childhood, or perhaps he would have let it slide. He was, after all, the kind of man who gave a tree to itself. William Henry aside, this article in the Banner is the first mention of the Tree, the love, the deed. No one else who had known William Henry was still alive at the time of the article, and no one else has ever claimed to have seen the deed but for this anonymous newspaper reporter who wrote the front page story quoting from it.

In 1906, George Foster Peabody, a supporter of Women's suffrage and African-American education, paid to have new soil and a fence built around the failing Tree, and the faithful local newspapers reported on it again. Peabody, it seems now, was the thoughtful soul who carved the words of the deed into the marble stone that stands as proof to the love that Jackson had for the Tree. The words engraved in the stone were taken from the story that ran in the Banner on August 12th, 1890, sixteen years earlier. It was a kind gesture to love, and interesting that Peabody had thought about the Tree and that newspaper article for sixteen years, though no one is certain of why he cared so much about it to begin with. Perhaps he just loved a good love story. Regardless, the Tree suffered during an ice storm shortly after Peabody's work on it, and heart rot and fungus and root infection took hold and nothing was done to save the Tree that was dying a slow and certain death, or so the Atlanta-Journal reported in 1937.

On October 9th, 1942, The Tree That Owns Itself fell. It was reported that the tired and worn oak dropped on a calm night, of its own volition. Because of wartime restrictions on reporting weather conditions, it could not be stated that the Tree actually came crashing down on that night due to rot and fungus and a violent wind storm.

The Tree That Owns Itself which stands on the corner of Dearing and South Finley now, with the bronze and marble plaques and the little fence is actually The Son of The Tree That Owns Itself. It was grown from an acorn of the original Tree and planted four years after its fall to take its place. In 1961, the Banner, which by then was the Banner-Herald, ran another story about the Tree. It credited Peabody's plaque and fence to William Henry and had him placing it there back in 1820.

The Son of the Tree That Owns Itself, still owns itself, though not actually legally. Legally, one must have the capacity to receive the thing that is being given. This stands to reason. If it did not, there is no telling what state of affairs all things would come to, while matters of ownership and history and fact would be subjected to any one person's wildly unreliable interpretation of them.

Moon Trees

THERE ARE CINNABAR TREES growing on the moon. They are somewhat smaller than the ones that grow on Earth because of the moon's lack of consistent rainfall, but they still grow in such profusion that when their leaves turn in autumn, the burning flame of red sets the entire face of the moon on fire and can be observed by the naked eye from Earth. Farmers of old worked by the thick blood-light of it hanging low on the horizon. They called it their Harvest Moon.

Cinnabar trees are also known as katsura. They are fast-growing trees, so long as the soil is deep and remains moist. But if it doesn't, the katsura has evolved to drop its pretty heart-shaped leaves and wait for the rains to return. If it has been a good year and the leaves are in plenty, come autumn they will ignite their green into red and the air will be filled with the warm scent of burnt brown sugar. This smell has been known to compel otherwise sensible women into extreme acts of adultery, and in some countries where katsura are abundant, women often cover themselves in sheets from head to foot, and ask their husbands to hide their car keys and to confine them to their homes during the autumnal months. Katsura are often grown as ornamental trees despite the grief they cause, for they are pendulous and prone to weeping. The katsura on the moon, however, are harmless to humans due to their great distance from Earth, and can be safely appreciated for their beauty.

It is probably obvious, but should be noted for clarity's sake, that the katsura are not native to the moon. They were planted there by the man who lives on it, most commonly known as "The Man in the Moon." Like the katsura, The Man in the Moon is not native to it. He was exiled there by Moses for gathering sticks in the wilderness on the Sabbath (Numbers 15:32–36). In those days, the man was called Mamre, which means rebellious; bitter; set with trees. After being discovered with his bundle of firewood, he was taken by Moses and the entire assembly to the outskirts of camp where he was to be stoned to death for breaking the Sabbath. There is some debate as to when this might have been. Rabbinical Judaism situates Moses' life between 1391–1271 BCE, while Eusebius Sophronius Hieronymus (St. Jerome) calculates that Moses' death was in 1592 BCE, and James Ussher (Ireland's famous scholar, archbishop and chronologer) has figured the year of his death to be 1619 BCE. Regardless, Mamre was not stoned to death as anticipated. The desert rocks were flung at him with such force that they lifted him from the ground and he shot through the sky holding fast to the bundle of katsura still gathered in his arms.

It appears that Mamre passed over China and Japan in his flight, and some of the winged seeds hidden in the branches fluttered down like pink cabbage moths and landed in good soil. That is how katsura came to thrive in these lands, though they died out later in Egypt after the plague of grasshoppers that the Lord sent the Pharaoh. After this accidental "planting" in Asia, Mamre eventually landed on the moon, and because there was no way back and nowhere else to go, he made it his home. He still carries his bundle of sticks every night as a warning to over workers, and when the moon is full, he can be seen silhouetted on the face of it.

The Man in the Moon is not the kind to be restricted by expectations, as proven by his original name and his Sabbath-breaking, and though he has been exiled, he has grown elegant and handsome in the passing years. It has been said that women should avoid looking at him directly, for he is lonely on the moon, tending his forest of red trees, and if he is in a bad temper, he will steal their souls.

It has also been said that he has both a fickle and charitable heart, and that when the mood strikes him, he gazes down on these women and is sometimes overcome by generous feelings. If this is the case, then he will unravel from his red silken coat a long thread. From his place on the moon, he is able to stitch it to the liver of a woman with one end and to the throat of a man with the other end. And when the time is right, he will pull. They will be drawn to each other, and nothing will prevent their union.

But the Man in the Moon changes faces often. Though he presents himself as a gentleman, keeping his shoes well shined and serving excellent wine with roast rabbit, he cannot be trusted. The astronauts who have flown to the moon know this to be true. He was offered communion and repentance when Apollo 11 first landed, but the Man in the Moon refused it. There is an article on this that is worth reading in the September 13th, 2012, edition of The Guardian entitled "How Buzz Aldrin's Communion on the Moon was Hushed Up."

In the spirit of reconciliation, or in the spirit of science surpassing God's wrath, Stuart Roosa of Apollo 14 brought The Man in the Moon tree seeds. Katsura are beautiful, but even beautiful things can become tiresome if there is nothing else to compare them to, and so Roosa packed five varieties for the journey: loblolly pine, sycamore, sweetgum, redwood, Douglas fir. They were donated to Roosa for his journey by the Forestry Service because prior to flying to the moon, Roosa flew into burning forests. He worked as a Smoke Jumper and launched himself out of planes and into raging wildfires below and so developed an affinity for trees through protecting them.

It is uncertain as to whether Roosa was most drawn to the forest or the fire or the moon. There are stories told by his mother of the way he reached for the rising globe in the window from his crib, as if it were a fruit to be bitten, and how he set fire to kites at night and let them loose into the black like a rocket blazing, though none of these have been verified.

Roosa, however, was not chosen to walk on the surface of the moon, but to orbit it alone as the other two astronauts pressed their rippled boot prints against its face. He circled it for two days, thirty-four times around, while five hundred seeds vibrated jealously in a vial beside him. "Space travel doesn't change you," Roosa said on return. "You bring back from the moon what you took to it." But how would he know? He wasn't allowed to set foot on it.

Upon returning home and during the decontamination process, the vial of seeds that had sat by his side for the entire trip exploded, and five hundred black tear drops scattered through the air and mixed together. The seeds were presumed dead.

They were planted anyway, in plastic trays of black dirt mixed with peat moss, divided into cubes of possible life, watered and charted and tracked by curious scientists. And then four-hundred-fifty little green heads sprouted from the soil, looking for the moon. The biggest surprise being that there was no surprise—that the trees grew at the same rate and health as any other tree. A loblolly pine was eventually planted at the White House; one was given to the Emperor of Japan; a Douglas fir to Flagstaff Junior. High; a sycamore to Camp Koch Girl Scout Camp in Indiana. They called them Moon Trees, and used ceremonial shovels tied with bright red ribbons to plant them in city squares and parks and universities.

For reasons now unclear, hundreds of the tiny saplings were delivered to Humboldt State University and sat in the greenhouses there for years, until no one remembered where they had come from to begin with or what they had once known. The trees became a nuisance, spindly and reaching and taking up space, so they were divided from one another, given to friends, planted alongside Earth trees and used for ornamentation on suburban lots, to mark boundary lines or to shade children's shallow wading pools. The trees that could not be given away were scattered throughout the campus, unmarked. And as they were forgotten they were lost to encroaching underbrush, bulldozers, housing expansions.

Moon Trees, unlike katsura, do not fill the air with the smell of burnt brown sugar in the fall or burst into bleeding-hearted foliage; they grow quietly, as most trees do. You could climb the branches of one, cut it down, and watch the sap bleed, build a house of its timber and live inside its wood without ever knowing of its journey into outer space. "The majority of people I know have no idea what they are or that we even have them," a student at Humboldt said. It is unclear if knowing would make any difference. They were, after all, known at one point and then left to be forgotten.

The moon doesn't care about any of this. It never has. The would-be first astronauts of Apollo 1 were once strapped to their seats for a launch pad test while orange flames licked their command module clean. The fire ate the flesh off their faces and arms and legs and stomachs until what was left were oily smudges inside space suits. The moon observed all this, but remained unmoved. Had it not, it surely would have drawn near to save them.

The Man in the Moon watched these attempts on Earth and wondered what the trouble was for. The moon was cold and lonely and made of the same stuff as the planet these men were trying to leave.

For every one of the thirty-four orbits that Roosa made around the moon, he spent forty-five minutes on the dark side of it, out of contact with mission control, cut off from the astronauts below and more alone than anyone at any time walking over the surface of the Earth.

The dark side of the moon is not dark but only hidden from our view. It glows red in the sunrise like a forest of katsura in flame. The Man in the Moon has seen this. He watched Roosa's pale face pass over it and felt the presence of the seeds above him. Who knows what impulses to unclick and jump might fill the mind of a man so alone? What stories he tells to anchor himself fast to the Earth below?

Rot

SQUIRRELS ARE NORTH AMERICA'S answer to the monkey, I think. I spend a lot of time sitting at my desk, looking out at the maple in the yard, distracted by their leaping of impossible distances to thin branches and then catching and swinging to safety. They holler and chase each other up and down the tree trunk, flying to the roof of my house, clinging with skinny fingers to gutters, and running back down the wall. I've even seen one climb the stairs on the swing set and try out the slide. It popped for joy like a happy toddler when it landed. In the spring, squirrels get busy making squirrel babies in the branches, and there is so much twisting and grabbing and open-mouthed ecstasy I look away and get busy shuffling my papers.

There was a dead one beneath the maple this spring, stretched out as if reaching, long and whole and seemingly unhurt with its eyes open, but very, very dead. I wanted to believe that he'd fallen in the throes of passion—one overly eager thrust and down he went to his lusty death, but when I asked, the Wildlife Department said that one third of squirrels die of starvation within the first year of their lives. In spring, sex and starvation go hand in hand.

Eastern Grey squirrels can be up to thirty centimeters long without their tails—which are another twenty-five centimeters long. And they weigh up to six-hundred grams, so a dead squirrel is substantial. It requires action: phone calls to the city or graves in the garden or at the very least scooping it up with a shovel and throwing it in the trash. But I was busy this spring, and not sure what I wanted to do, and quickly forgot about the body on my lawn.

Nature, however, knows exactly what to do. As soon as an animal's heart stops beating, the chemicals in its body change and so its pH levels change and so its cells lose their structural integrity. They sway and crash like an old house in the wind. Cellular enzymes spill free from the wreckage and begin to eat away at the other cells and tissues, releasing more enzymes, more crashing, more destruction. Scientists call this autolysis: self-digestion. It comes from two Greek words meaning "self-splitting". As if bodies carry inside themselves the potential to undo themselves. Catch a squirrel by the tail and it'll fall off, though it won't grow a new one.

That bodies so readily turn on themselves after death can almost be forgiven by the way they so readily recreate. If a squirrel survives its first year of life, it will most likely live for another twelve-and-a-half years and start reproducing when it is a year old. It'll have somewhere between two to eight babies, twice a year, born naked, toothless, and blind. But if they don't starve there is still the possibility they'll be eaten by hawks or owls or snakes or raccoons or skunks or cats or bored stray dogs. They might fall out of a maple and die on the new spring lawn. Nature lurks around the edges of home, killing and birthing at random.

For two or three days, there was no noticeable change in my squirrel. It was the car crash syndrome every time I walked past—I wanted to look, but I was afraid I'd see white worms crawling out of its mouth or rot exploding from its stomach. But the squirrel only grew noticeably fatter, like he had been sitting around eating peanuts and watching TV instead of being dead all day. He was filling with something, until the warm spring afternoon when an insect ate the fur off of it in bunches, and some animal picked its eyes out.

The schedule of rot, I read, is divided into five stages: Fresh, Bloat, Active Decay, Advanced Decay, and Dry Remains. These are fairly self-explanatory terms. Especially Bloat. A body in the Bloat stage looks bloated. Tissues liquefy and become frothy. The abdomen distends, fluids escape the built-up pressure of gases through the nose, mouth, anus. Sometimes the skin ruptures. Blowflies can smell rotting flesh from ten miles away. Their maggots feed under the surface, and the skin becomes a loose robe, detached, hair falling out in chunks. The seeping fluids create a "cadaver decomposition island" (CDI). A circle of death surrounds the dead; the grasses die, flies gather, maggots multiply. The smell of rot is the smell of the body purging itself of control.

Once I found a baby chickadee on the sidewalk with its head burrowed under its wing. I was on my way for ice cream when I saw it huddled there with a crow squawking overhead. No nests nearby, and the bird was only half-feathered, half down, so I scooped it up and carried it home in my hands. It tweeted back at another chickadee on the walk. It pooped on my palms. I decided to nurse it through the night and call the wildlife rescue people in the morning. I sat on the couch with it snuggled on my chest, kept it warm, and tried to feed it water from my finger. It wouldn't eat worms. Or aphids. I named her Thief for her black mask and wrapped fleece around her. Close to midnight, a sweet smell started wafting off her feathers. In the morning she was dead. I've heard that bluebottle flies can smell death coming and swarm before it happens, but scientists say it's just a story. I buried her tiny body in the flower garden. It only took a minute.

The squirrels' maple grows in the flower garden along with an elm and gingko biloba, and all three trees are continually encroaching on the lawn. They drop seeds or send out suckers and push against their allotted spaces. By the end of the summer I have substantially less lawn and more forest than I did in the spring. If I didn't uproot all the saplings there would be nothing but trees in two or three years. They will eat up Thief's body in one tiny bite like a midnight snack. They are merciless in their growth.

I start noticing the edges of things, the way perimeters are consumed and rot runs on a schedule, the way control is temporary and the possibility of chaos flutters around the edges of home like a moth against the windows. It isn't only the body's decay that waits in the wings to pounce—that one is obvious, we all know what comes for us in the end—but it is the loosening of anchors, the slip-up into no return that worry me most. The man on the sidewalk who holds out a cracked palm as I pass is not the elected poor. He wanders into city hall and sits at the grand piano and plays until you weep. And the woman downtown in the pale green cardigan who constantly asks for quarters used to teach in the philosophy department at the University of Alberta. I have friends who knew her then.

So I make my own damn schedules.

I keep my house clean. I buy fresh fruit. I finish my work on time no matter what, and I do not stop do notstopdonotstopdonot, because when you stop, cell walls collapse. Everything collapses. I don't have time to bury a rotting squirrel. But the dust keeps blowing in, settling down; my own dead skin cells sparkle in the sunlight, raining onto all my polished furniture. At night I lie in bed and feel the thinness of the boundaries I've made.

I've lived in this house for two years now and watched the seasons force the maple into cycles of bloom and beauty and death and nakedness, but who needs another tree metaphor about change and weathering the storms and remaining beautiful through it all? A tree is not a metaphor. A tree is a tree, and we are both only one strong wind away from falling. Our bodies already know how to begin. I tied a pretty ribbon around the maple in the bare months to ease its despair, because some morning, I might stay in bed for a year or two. Some days, I let a squirrel rot on the lawn; I lean towards immobility; I practice falling in tiny ways.

The first autumn here I bought a rake and gardening gloves and piled the bright leaves into black plastic bags while the squirrels screeched at me overhead. The air was sweet with the smell of green things turning and winter encroaching, but I burned my nose in the sun and took off my sweater in the heat. At least ten bags full of leaves. It took me all afternoon, though the schedule said to buy groceries, read, clean, fold laundry, go to the library. All the bags hauled and piled neatly at the curb looked like a good day's work, like order and business taken care of. All of the houses, all of the neighbors' bags down the street sat at the curbs, pictures of suburban stability, waiting patiently for the garbage truck to take them away from us. It came two days later and the men tossed all the bags into the back, but when they came to mine, they moved along.

Leaves are not trash, I learned, and if I wanted them gone I had to use paper bags, not plastic. So I dragged them all back to the yard and piled them against the side of the house where I wouldn't see them until I had time to do something about it. But first, I'd have to buy the proper bags, I'd have to transfer them all, I'd have to find out when another yard waste pickup day was, and then I'd have to haul them all back to the curb.

But there was the schedule, and there was still cleaning to do and books to read and groceries to buy, and then one night it snowed. And then it snowed some more, and then there was no yard waste pickup scheduled for a very long time.

Spring exploded miraculously the way it always does, with that strange bright baby green of sticky new leaves and red tulips and hairy crocuses. The plastic bags sat by the side of the house throughout that spring, and then all of a sudden it was summer, and then I was gone for holidays, and then I was home, and then it was autumn again. I raked up the new leaves and brought them to the curb, but the old ones stayed where they were.

Sometimes, I walked to the side of the house to check on them. Mice and squirrels had bitten holes in them, branches poked through the slumping plastic, a circle of rotting dead grass surrounded them. Some nights I couldn't sleep. I waited for the neighbor on the trashy side of the house to complain. I waited to be fined. I worried about animals that might eat the plastic. I worried what it meant that I couldn't take care of this one little thing. But I left the leaves there, for nearly two years.

And then one spring day I woke up and walked to the hardware store down the block. I rented a mulching lawnmower and wheeled it home with brown paper bags for leaves tucked under my arm, and I mowed the hell out of my lawn. I trimmed the overgrown flower beds, took down the saplings and beat back the encroaching growth. When I finished, there were edges separating flowers from lawn, sidewalk from ferns, a stack of neatly piled maple branches that had fallen during windstorms, and brown paper bags filled with grass and weeds and dried lily stocks. I put a Band Aid over the weeping blister on my thumb, grabbed another paper bag that was nearly as tall as me, and walked to the side of the house.

I imagined I would find mice nests snuggled into the leaves, filled with blind pink babies. I imagined snakes. And salamanders. And all the things that thrive in the musty dark of decay. I put on my gloves and cut open the top of the first bag.

A fat earth worm wiggled on a bed of black dirt, another pale leggy bug skittered away into a dark hole. It smelled like a wet forest. At the bottom of the bag there was only more black dirt, frightened bugs, a few tree branches that hadn't yet decomposed. In two years there was nothing left of the maple leaves. I took bag after bag and dumped the dirt into flower beds, spreading the old leaves out with the rake that had piled them into bags two autumns ago. The maple will eat them up and spend the winter knitting buds. Next spring, there will be leaves again. Even children know this, though it is no less astounding. Sometimes rot is gracious.

Autolysis means that I live in a body ready to eat my own body, and that I exist inside the continual possibility of being split from myself. Once, when my once respectable father had started smoking crack, I thought I saw him stumble in front of my car as I stopped at a crosswalk. Who needs another tree metaphor? One morning I woke up and the rotten squirrel was just gone.

Inosculation

The Journal of Axel Erlandson

Minnesota, January 1, 1900
Average Precipitation per Month

	(Inches)
January	0.32
February	0.22
March	1.98
April	2.51
May	1.11
June	6.12
July	4.91
August	1.48
September	1.24
October	3.55
November	0.70
December	0.77

There's a pile of my old notebooks stored in a cardboard box in the toolshed behind the house. The earliest one is from 1896 when I was twelve years old, and yesterday I pulled that box out and started flipping through some of them. Pages and pages of lists. I don't remember ever wondering why I always wanted to record everything, only that it seemed like someone needed to, as if these things wouldn't have existed if I hadn't written them down.

I never wrote many words down with my lists, just like I never said many words. They're mostly numbers with some small notations to make sense of what the numbers are referring to. This list beside me of screws and wood and equipment that I bartered work for is from the September I was sixteen and spent my evenings in the barn building a model threshing machine. The journal still smells like hay. I don't know how that could be, but it does. And when I smell that smell, I remember tightening those bolts in a warm barn on a fall night with the frogs calling from the dark in a pond the horses drink from. Just like that. I remember those things.

I was supposed to be working the kilns with my brothers and father, but some nights when my heart had been bothering me all day, my mother would take my chin in her hands and stare into my eyes. I mean, stare. Look right into the back of my head, and she would know my heart had been giving me a pain and she'd make me stay home. So I went to the barn and worked instead. I hated it when she did that, but those kilns were fierce on my heart and would have probably killed me young.

My mother always said that her boys were meant to be farmers, and she was happiest at the sight of all three of us coming in from the field with dirt on our necks and in the curls of our ears. One night I walked back to the house from the barn and told my mother to come. I remember that I opened the kitchen door for her to the yard and there were stars scattered as thick as a seeded field over us. Of course, there were stars. There were always stars, but that night I took in the sight of them and we walked through the yard under their cold light, past the garden and sleeping chickens, to the wide red doors of the barn and to the miniature thresher I had finally finished building. She laughed when I turned the wheel and grain came tumbling out into her hand.

But it is hard to say if that is how it really went. My mind rewrites itself over the years, and when I think on it, I remember that our barn was never red.

When we rented a train car the next year to move from northwestern Minnesota to the San Joaquin Valley in California, I was not allowed to take my thresher. I dug a hole next to the pond and buried it like a body.

The journals from our first years in California are records of nothing rather than something. Lists of no rain, of no money, of failed crops. And then, when irrigation came to the valley, a great swath of time and abundance of pages when I purchased a surveyor's level and filled my notebook with soil measurements

and mathematical equations, stake heights and the dirt move-
ment that was necessary for irrigation on our farms. It's all very
boring to read now. I spent some hours flipping through those
pages, but none of it means anything anymore. It reminds me of
those cave paintings they sometimes find in the hills—all those
recorded moments with no path back to what they once meant.
But at least the paintings are beautiful. I should throw my journals out. But I don't want to. When I am dead, someone will
come along and burn the lot, I'm sure, and I'll never have to
know about it. Besides, there are a few lists I want to read again.

> First blackbird of the year: March 4th, 1901
> First rainfall of the spring: March 7th, 1901
> First blooming crocuses: April 14th, 1901
> Spring barley crops planted: May 17, 1901
> Barley crops harvested: August: 29, 1901
> First snowfall of the year: November 5th, 1901

I used to spend a lot of time in the woods. It's been years since
I've walked in them, and now that I can hardly stand, all I want is
the smell of an autumn forest and to watch the tiny birds' nests
appear like bald secrets in the trees. A forest is a secret, I guess.
As much as another person is. Maybe that is what I was doing
with all these lists. Maybe they weren't as much about knowing
the world, as admitting to not knowing. Lists of the things that
managed to surprise me. I am not sure if my soul has ever been

large enough to contain such a generosity as that, but I want to think it possible, even if I did not know it at the time.

Some of these old lists are about love—the qualities I expected in a wife, what I thought she should look like, even the kind of meals she would make for me. And all of this from a time when I didn't have the courage to speak to any of the women I knew. By the time I was thirty, I decided that marriage to any woman would work out all right if I had the right mindset, if I could let commitment rule over all the rest of me. I thought love should be sensible. So I wrote to a woman in St. Louis at an address that a friend gave me.

Courtship through mail suited me best. It must have suited her, too. Leona sent me a picture of herself after my first letter to her, assuming, I guessed, that it would be what I was most interested in knowing. So I put on my Sunday suit and took a ride with a neighbor into town. I had my picture taken at the photography studio, one with my hat on and one without. I remembered to keep my mouth closed and was pleased with the result. I tucked the photograph into an envelope, and, feeling confident, remembered the weekly poem printed in the newspaper. I clipped it out and sent it along too, as if it were some sort of concession to romance. I copied it into my notebook. Here it is. A month later I was on a train to St. Louis to meet and marry her.

My notebooks from our first years of marriage are painful to read even now. Leona was plain and shy—a bit of an old maid, and I was a silent and moody bachelor. She was not a quick wit, but neither was I, and she seemed kind enough. She had a settled air of steadfastness around her that both pleased and irritated me. Sometimes on sunny days when I worked in the yard, she would carry her wash tub out of doors and I'd watch her scrub clothes along the ribbed board, arms red and splotchy from the scalding water right up to the elbows. She seemed ancient to me like that, as if she had been washing clothes in that bucket for five thousand years, watching the world turn from her seat on the stump.

We were poor, and though I had written these lists my entire life, Leona took my recording of the money she spent as a reproach to her. When we fought about it, I pulled out years of old notebooks and shoved them under her nose to prove my innocence, though I am not certain now that she was wrong in her accusations. I was so used to being alone, to deciding the how and when of everything. I didn't understand the twisted roads my arguments took with her—why I couldn't bring myself to say the simple truth of anything. "We have no money and I am afraid," or "You still do not love me and I am sorry for that." It would have been so much better, but there was no speaking of anything true in those days, only self-protection. No tenderness between us. No mercy. She cried in the cellar sitting on sacks of potatoes, and I closed the door so as not to hear her.

My recordings during these years are more sporadic than others, as if in not writing them down they might undo themselves. She left me one day a few years in. I saw her going, though she didn't know it. Walking back from town with a replacement disc for the plow, I stood in the ditch to let a buggy pass and saw her wet face ride by me and knew what it meant.

It's funny, the things you do when life goes wrong. I went home, took an apple, and cut it into quarters, sat at the table and ate each slice slowly. I remember the crunch of the flesh in my mouth and the ticking of the clock in the front room were the only sounds. I sat for a long time, until it grew dark, then I gathered the seeds and tucked them in the pocket of my overalls. It suddenly seemed wrong to waste a thing with life in it.

The Psalmist says that salvation comes in the morning. I don't know about that, but the sun does anyway, and I went for a walk in the woods when it did. I walked in the woods with my head all cottony from the night, looking for a place to plant the apple seeds, and I found a tree that I had not seen before. It was a sycamore, or, rather, two sycamores. They had sprouted independently, but so close to one another that they had fused and formed one trunk. The seam between them was grotesque, like the scar from an infected wound, and it dipped and bulged as if there were boils blooming beneath it. But it must have been this shape, or death. The larger might have strangled the smaller, but instead they grew and pushed and rubbed the bark off their trunks until they were raw and weeping, until they grew into something misshapen and singular.

I didn't plant the apple seeds. I found some paste and glued them to my notebook, then drove out to St. Louis and brought Leona back. I don't know why she came, but she stayed, still stays. There is one shriveled apple seed left from that day, stuck to the page like a black beetle under glass.

After Leona came home, our marriage settled into something even quieter than it had been. It was not better, but it was all we knew to do, and so we worked and waited for the thing that would come along and save us. I planted and harvested; she cooked and cleaned. The years passed.

I thought a lot about those sycamores in those days and their ugly bodies, how nature does not concern itself with beauty, that all things beautiful are a happy accident of practicality. I found that if I made tiny slices on the bark of two young saplings and then tied them together, they would grow into one another like the sycamores in the forest. After some time, I thought that it might be possible to force the trees into strange or pleasing shapes, and I began sketching pictures of what I thought they might become in my notebooks.

By then, Leona was busy with our baby, Wilma, and I found myself hovering around the house like a lonely ghost in the evenings, so I'd take off outside and draw out my tree plans at night, as if I were sixteen again and working alone in the barn.

Of course, I couldn't know for two, three, four years whether or not the trees would take to my shaping, since working with trees is such a slow-going process, but every day I would farm and my mind would be with the trees, and then after dinner I would clip and scrape and bind them together.

I've got nearly forty years' worth of working with the trees recorded in these books. This one here has the plans to the Poplar Archway penciled inside it: I used ten trees to make it, measuring fifteen feet across in total, with each tree spaced eighteen inches apart, and a three-foot divide in the middle to walk through. At three feet high, the trees were to split and join with the tree beside it. It looked like a wall of stained-glass window, I thought. I wanted it to grow to be about twenty feet tall. Leona and I fought about that one. I think my trees embarrassed her sometimes. I know some of her friends thought they were awful, like a deformed child with bits of beauty that made its ugliness even more shameful.

I can still make out my writing on the plans for the Poplar Archway. "I believe I can get a tree to grow like this illustration. December 8th, 1929." On the right side of the picture, Leona has written, "I do not believe that Axel can get a tree to grow like this illustration." She's signed and dated it, too.

I grew it exactly how I wanted it to, and big enough that I could stand under the archway with two feet to spare above me. I don't remember any satisfaction in proving myself to Leona, or even the moment of showing the finished archway to her. I guess it would have been obvious long before the trees matured that I had done what she thought I couldn't. In the same way I had watched her spend her money so carefully, she had watched me spend my time.

I kept experimenting. My notes are full of the designs I drew at night while Leona did mothering things. I made diamond-shaped trees, cathedral-shaped trees, a bird cage, a ladder, a zigzag, a telephone booth, a spiral, a heart, a tree with a knot in it—twenty years' worth of evenings, sitting in the barn drawing plans and building forms to direct the trees. I do not know if I was ever wanted in the house; it never occurred to me that I could belong there. But I felt the lack of Leona and Wilma. Or the lack of something, at least. Maybe I named it them because it was the easiest thing to hope for, a thing that could still be had. Every night I imagined them opening the workshop door to step in from the dark, smelling of the warmth of the house, of dinner and that soap they used, and to ask me what I was so busy doing with the trees.

One night, Wilma did come. She must have been thirteen or fourteen. I don't remember anymore. What I do remember is that she seemed like a stranger from church to me. A face I knew enough to smile at, but nothing more. She stood beside me in the workshop and I could see the little hairs standing straight on her arms from the cold, the clean curl of her ear and a hangnail on her thumb, ripped and tender, a little dried blood at the edges that I wanted to wrap with a white piece of cotton. She was so beautiful to me, but I didn't know how to say it.

She wanted me to teach her how to grow the trees into shapes, and had a little sycamore sapling of her own that she wanted to work on. It didn't go so well. I gave her a notebook to draw her plans in, but she didn't want a notebook. So I told her about the sycamore I had first seen growing in the forest. She listened, and I could tell that she wanted something from me, that she was collecting my words to keep for later, like picking apples off a tree, and it hurt me to see that, to see her so hungry for my words. So I stopped talking. I tried to show her instead by working on the trees, but I don't think she understood. She thought I was keeping things from her, keeping my tree secrets away from her. She came out to watch me work a few more evenings and tried to bend her sycamore around an old frame that I had made for a poplar once, but her tree snapped and she stayed in the house from then on in.

Regret is too harsh of a word to use when I don't know how things could have ever turned out differently: Leona and Wilma being who they were, me being me.

I have a book in here of Chinese horticulture that Wilma gave me for Christmas one year. It's not much good since we don't live in China, but no one ever knows what to get a seventy-nine-year-old man for Christmas. There is one useful thing that I've found in it though. It says that Classic Chinese poetry is written in four lines. The first line presents the subject, the second explains it further, the third line introduces an unrelated thought, and then the fourth line explains the connection between them all. If my life were a poem, the trees would be the third line. I like to think about that sometimes.

One summer, when Wilma was seventeen, I think, she took a trip to Santa Cruz with Leona. A farmer can't vacation in the summer, even if he wants to, so I stayed to work. Leona came back talking about some roadside attraction she'd seen. Hundreds of people stopped in to see this place called The Mystery Spot, and how they made you believe in magic, how the sloped walls had made her feel as though she were standing on the walls of a house. "It's too bad you never take vacations," she said. "You should put your trees in something like that."

"Yes," I said. "Maybe I should. I'll think on it," to which she raised her shoulders for a moment and then smiled and walked away. I did think on it—it and nothing else. I started to imagine my trees out in public, I thought of the things the people would say, how amazed everyone would be at their strange and beautiful shapes, how they must seem to others as exotic and wonderful as trapeze women flying through the air at a circus. I began to dream of them being seen by hundreds of people, how right that would be, how like a reward to a life of hard and quiet work it would be.

One evening that October, when the last of the black-eyed beans were in from the field and ready to ship, I found Leona sitting in the kitchen reading at the table alone, and I said all at once, "Let's sell the farm and plant my trees by the roadside." She blinked at me behind her round black glasses and waited. She had always been plump and soft-waisted, but the last few years had been kind to her in a way that they had held back from me. She looked sweet in her age and had laugh lines around her mouth, though I could not think of hearing her laugh. "I'm sixty," I said, "and everything tastes like field dust and sand."

That winter, we talked of nothing but the trees. I stayed inside at night with my notebooks and showed them my plans for the saplings that were still growing and for the trees that I hadn't planted yet. We took out old photos from a Sunday afternoon when Wilma was still a little girl and I had lifted her up and snuggled her in the curves of one of my trees. We would use those pictures for postcards in the souvenir shop, we decided. Leona said we'd need to build a tall fence to keep people out and so we priced out the cost of it, and I wrote figures for the moving trucks and hired help. Before the year was over I had purchased three quarters of an acre of land in Scotts Valley. We left the farm. I quit farming. We moved everything out.

During the weeks we spent preparing the trees for the move, the farm was filled with people trimming and digging, trucks backing into the yard and my enormous trees pulled up from the dirt, roots dangling like loose teeth. Leona helped me wrap the bare ends in peat moss and burlap, and I built a winch to lift them onto the flatbeds.

It is hard to say if my wife has ever loved me. I don't know anymore what that might mean. We learned to live around each other and to depend on the other, but during those weeks it was as if we were shown the thing we could have been, as if we were people in a poem, carrying each other's heart inside our old bodies like a secret from everyone else. I wanted it all over again. I wanted my youth and violin-playing, I wanted time to send more pictures in the mail and the early years back and reading by lamplight at night and a house full of babies—not just one—and words to say what needed speaking, not writing. I wanted to squeeze the flesh at her waist until she laughed and pushed me from her.

World's Strangest Trees!

Visitor Log

1947	108 people
1948	402 people
1949	278 people
1950	498 people
1951	415 people
1952	597 people
1953	307 people
1954	105 people
1955	37 people
1956	12 people
1957	4812 people
1958	2832 people
1959	2233 people
1960	3567 people
1961	3389 people
1962	3925 people
1963	3533 people

Wilma changed the name to the Tree Circus a few years after we opened, and I liked that. The idea of them being surrounded by acts of wonder and wild animals and rings of fire seemed right. They appeared in Life magazine once, and in Ripley's Believe It Or Not!, too. I grew another seventy-five trees once we opened. I imagined someday being able to walk through an entire forest of wonder, where what I imagined shaped the way things turned out. When the pictures came out in Life and Ripley's we rode that wave of happiness for a while, until the numbers hovered at a high and then began to drop. After some time, we knew it had been as good as it ever would be.

I didn't leave the grounds much after that. I couldn't leave my trees. It was terrible to think of someone coming to see them and finding the gates locked, so I stayed. With every visitor I recorded, and some days there were none at all, some weeks, I thought that this might be the person who would see something different in my trees, something that wasn't so much like a freak show. I thought it could be love. Once, a small child asked me how I got the trees to grow as they did, and I told her that I talked to them.

Wilma and Leona moved out two years ago. I've been living in the back of the souvenir shop since then. It's shaped like a castle made of gigantic stones, but of course it's only painted plywood. I sold my trees for $12000 to a theme park called The Lost World because the farm was gone and no one comes to visit me here anymore. The Lost World has life-sized dinosaurs made of fiberglass scattered throughout the property now. The owners are nice enough; they let me stay on as a groundskeeper and once in a while I see someone leaving with a postcard of me standing beneath the Poplar Arch when it was still young and growing and Wilma was beside me as a little girl in short socks.

I had to bring my notebooks in from the workshop. They needed the space to build a Triceratops. I've been looking through them, wondering what to do with it all. I can't make any sense of the lists anymore. They aren't even beautiful. What are they for?

Artifacts

Whatever the desert wants is of the desert.
—Tuareg proverb

The Green Sahara

Sand remembers the sun and stores the sight of it away inside itself. The paleontologists know the nature of the sand. They dig in the dark on a moonless night in Niger so as not to spoil the light inside the grains; they dig through dunes, down deep to the bottom of an ancient lake, and scoop samples of it up into tiny black jars that will fly over the sea and to another country, where the history of light will be pulled from the grains and given a date: fifteen thousand years ago the sun shone on these sands.

The sand's memory is as deep as the sand is. It pockets away souvenirs in its folds like a child pocketing shells on a beach. Hidden just below the shifting surfaces are the bones of a square-nosed Nigersaurus, a crocodile-jawed Suchominus and an Ouranosaurus or Brave Monitor Lizard. "Brave" because courage is necessary to survive the desert.

Sand has pushed against the boundaries of green for millennia. It ate the swamplands of the dinosaurs, the lush watersheds of the rhinoceros and hippopotamus, the grasslands of the giraffe. One third of the Earth is desert, one fifth of that is sand. It has grown and stretched unimpeded for the last seventy thousand years in the Sahara, except for a small hiccough of time when the Earth wobbled on its axis and monsoons wandered off course. Then, trees and grasses and flowers sprouted up where once was only desert, and animals followed the path of the waters and the people followed the path of the meat.

During the day, after the paleontologists have caught up on some sleep from their night digging, they shuffle through the dunes with their tiny brushes and notebooks, and the sun heats the air to 108 degrees. They have been kneeling in the desert for months already, labeling and molding and collecting their finds of varied 'sauruses, while armed Nigerien guards play with the guns that are strapped to their sides like babies. The desert is still a place that requires courage.

One day, a photographer from the team rises from his knees and adjusts his hat. There is sand collecting in the curves of his ears, sand in his neck, in his socks between his toes, sand grinding between his teeth. Sand in his hair, sand in his underwear, sand, real sand, in the corners of his eyes. He turns from the site and from the flick of bristle brush against dried bones and sets off for a nearby rise. The guards watch him leave and follow him with their eyes.

The threat of erupting violence is even more oppressive than the heat. The photographer climbs up a dune and slides down the other side, but he won't wander far. He's seen how easy it is to turn once, twice, cross a dune and lose all sense of direction.

The wind picks up for a moment and the desert changes its slithering face before him until he is blinded by it. He lifts a cloth to his mouth and nose, closes his eyes, breathes through the fabric and waits for it to pass. There is no use in fighting it. When the wind dies down and the dust settles back, he lowers the cloth and opens his eyes. Over the rise, he assumes, the group is still brushing madly at the dinosaurs, but at his feet, a human hand rises up through the sand like a blossom of bone. He shouts as loudly as he can, not wanting to leave it for even a moment for the sand to reclaim.

They uncover nearly two hundred human bodies that have been tucked into the ground for eight thousand years. They are the remains of the people of the Green Sahara—those who lived inside the monsoon miracle of a lush desert. They name the place Gobero.

Whatever seriousness or sorrows these Green Sahara people must have faced in life, they abandoned in death. Their bones seem joyful. There is a man found riding a tortoise, another with his head in a pot, a woman wearing a bracelet of hippo tusk. Their skulls are colored golden, and their teeth are white and straight and beautiful though they are ground down to the nerve from the sand in their food.

The paleontologists find pots and bowls and dishes and jewelry and old fires and animal bones and clothes that crumble when they are touched. The evidence of lives that so resemble their own is unnerving. They are used to unearthing dinosaur bones.

They uncover a favorite. She is a young mother buried on her side, facing her two little girls. Their legs are draped over each other and their hands all clasped together on a bed of yellow wool flowers.

"These people loved one another," the paleontologists say to the reporters who have come for the story. It shouldn't be surprising, they know, and yet it is. There is such tenderness in the way the mother cares for her girls in death, and in the way her babies reach out to her for comfort. But it is also the presence of the unknown fourth party—the living one who had been left behind and placed the bodies in the grave with such care that makes it all appear so startlingly modern, so familiar, as if motherhood and family and love had not evolved in eight thousand years, and there had always been the same need to be touched and known and comforted. A man gently brushes the sand away from the hands of the mother and girls and prepares to lift them from the earth while the reporters record it all.

There are only small windows of time left to discover these forgotten people. The permit to dig here is running out and will not be approved for renewal. Overnight, the wind reburies what took the paleontologists hours to unearth, and the desert rearranges itself, tucking its children back into bed while they sleep.

L'Arbre du Ténéré

When the acacia trees were in bloom; when the yellow-petaled masses of them exalted together crying "Nectar," crying "Flower," crying "Glory," when they hummed with the bees heavy in pollen; when they murmured to the turtledoves necking in their branches; when they called to the ant, gave their limbs to their houses; when the people of the desert climbed into their safe arms and were rocked to sleep alongside the birds, the acacia were fortresses of life. They were a garden of cool in the parched night and a kinder blooming star than the sun.

Though the sand crept closer every year like a spill across the desert floor, it did not terrify the living until the end had already begun. The desert had always known seasons of abundance and loss, patterns of rain and drought. So the first spring that the buds were killed in their casings before they could unfurl there was no fear, though the birds had lifted from their nests and had not returned. Above ground, the leaves curled and wilted on the branch, but below ground, the trees did what they had always done and sunk their tangled roots deeper into dark cold pools and waited.

But the sand could not be made to move in seasons anymore. It ate the spring and winter, ate the rains and shade, ate the blossoms, ate the fruit, it ate leaves and limbs and bark and all green things growing. The sand reached below ground and sucked the water from the secret streams, and everything died in time and nothing returned in time.

When there were no trees within sight, no trees within scent, within pollination, within four hundred kilometers of it, there remained a single stubborn acacia miraculously blooming in the desert—the Loneliest Tree in the World. But it was never so lonely as when its flowered branches cried out "Glory" on their own.

When years of solitude turned the Tree holy, the salt caravans, led by the Tuareg people, came to kneel beneath the Tree for prayers before they set off. Under the acacia they cried out "Mercy," cried out "Courage," cried out "Life!" Then they climbed their loaded camels and turned toward the city of Bilma and its ancient oasis of salt. The Tuareg navigated the shifting dunes by the unchanging things before them—by the sun and the stars and the Tree.

When the French colonialists came to Niger, came to the desert, came to the Tree, they watched the Tuareg bend and pray at the base of it. The Frenchmen shrugged, turned from the prayers and decided to sink a well beneath the Tree. If the Tree could survive, it was because it was drinking from some source, and how foolish of the thirsty Nigeriens not to have thought of this themselves, and this is why they needed them, to think of these things, and so they pulled men in from their work and told them to dig.

The sun dripped flames in the heat while the men shoveled through the sand and down to the white clay. They dug for hours and days, until they'd sunk so far they needed ropes to haul the earth over their heads to the ground above, and still no water.

A flock of turtledoves arrived and lighted on the branches of the Tree while the men worked. They cooed love songs and nuzzled necks as if they sat in the abundance of a forest instead of this last outpost of life. When the birds had rested, they lifted and left for the skies, and then flew out to a salt caravan plodding in the distance. The turtledoves circled the group, like seabirds following a doomed ship into the ocean.

The men struck water at 130 feet deep, and the acacia shrunk back against it. The Tree's small branches bloomed yellow for years after, and tiny glories were sent out into the emptiness, but every spring was quieter than the last. The caravans still paused their camels and prayed at the Tree, though they also grew fewer and smaller when truck caravans were used instead. The salt trucks stopped at the Tree, too, but only to suck up the water from its well. Once, a large limb was shorn off the tree when a truck backed into it. The limb was cut up and fed into the fire to heat the driver's tea.

When the Tree was naked, when it was blind and wounded, when it was silent in the season of flowers and silent in the season of fruit, when the birds would not nest in it and the ants had no use for it, when the people of the desert prayed at it but did not climb into its arms, the Tree felt the mouth of the desert open wide to swallow it whole. One night, a truck swayed drunkenly through the sand and crashed into the only thing standing for four hundred kilometers. The Tree fell to the ground dead, with a stubborn green vein still throbbing through its center.

Some government men came later and loaded the broken pieces of the famous trunk and limbs onto a flatbed. The Tree was glued back together in a city full of green trees. It was renamed L'Arbre du Ténéré—The Tree at the Heart of the Desert, and a picture of it was printed on commemorative stamps to celebrate its persistence in the face of inevitable death. It can be viewed behind a mesh fence at the Musée National du Niger, and in old photos collected under the heading The Loneliest Tree in the World.

The Bones

"You belong to the primate group called hominids," the exhibition in Chicago's Field museum of Natural History tells me. I have hands and feet that grasp, forward-facing eyes, and my closest ancestor is an ape. I am evolved for a life in the trees, and though it's been millions of years since we've lived in them, 89% of us still have the Palmaris muscle that runs from wrist to elbow to help us scramble up trunks and swing through the air. We also have wisdom teeth for chewing plants we no longer eat, and a small pink fold in the corner of our eyes that used to be a third eyelid.

The curved room is full of glass cases of bone or casts of bone and artifacts of our human evolution, dimly lit as if to soften the blow that we were once less sophisticated and much hairier than we are now.

Scientists, the display informs me, study the bones of the feet and pelvis to determine whether the animal remains they are holding stood and moved upright or if it clambered on all fours through branches in the sky and leaves. They study this, because this is what so much of the "ape" or "hominid" categorization hinges upon—the moment we climbed down from the trees and put one foot in front of only one other foot; this was when everything began to change for us.

In one of the glass cases, displayed by herself, is a ten-thousand-year-old woman who was mummified by the desert sand. She is buried in a pot in the fetal position, curled as tightly as the bud of a baby in a womb. It is as if those who laid her in the ground noticed that the best shape to take when transporting from one life to the next was a posture prepared for birth.

What I notice about her first is her teeth. Her skull is a little crumbly and cracked, and she looks so tiny without her skin and hardly hominoid, but her teeth are human teeth, familiar teeth, could be the teeth of anyone I might meet as I go throughout my day. They look like mine. This is unnerving. It is not so much because of the obvious reminder of my own impending death, but of the unrelenting machine of evolution. There is such a quietness that surrounds these millions of dead who have been fed into it, as if there were an endpoint goal that we were all being sacrificed to, but unknowingly, blindly. To look ten thousand years into the past begs a look to ten thousand years into the future, and it is incomprehensible to imagine what we might become, or why we should become anything at all. What is so wrong with apes? Why the constant need to evolve into something else? She seems so lonely in her little glass case.

The man I am with walks up to me and stares at the woman inside. "It's so strange," he says, "the way bones tell so little of a life." He puts his face into my hair in the near dark and says quietly into my ear, "I like to kiss your teeth. Her bones say nothing about anyone kissing her teeth."

I am ridiculous. I cry in a museum for a woman who has been dead ten thousand years, but I do it quietly, and the man I love doesn't notice; he holds my hand and reads a little more. There is no helping it anyway.

In another ten thousand years, all of what might remain of our time will be a spoon, a bowl, a cup, certainly a sediment layer of plastic only partially disintegrated and maybe a set of teeth rattling in a skull. My teeth are loved; when that is done, they will say nothing, because that is the deal we've been given and that is the way this works. It seems sensible, in light of these immutable facts, to forget all else.

Amor Fati

It is a dark night in the desert. A lone man comes to the stump of the Tree and begins to dig. He has brought what he can find—old mufflers and pipes and truck parts. He knows that the sand holds secrets, and that the people resting inside of it are waiting to be joined by others, so he works all night welding and fastening the pieces together in spite of this, because of it. In the morning, he raises up a new Arbre du Ténéré made of metal and aluminum. It is a monument to the place of departure, a reference to give scale to the size of the loss.

The desert is a memorial to loneliness made of sand and bone. The bones blow over the vast expanse and cry "Glory," cry "Loved," cry "Death." It is not that they need to be remembered; they are as numerous as the stars in the sky and as removed as those distant lights. But the bones were not always mile after mile of sand; once, someone loved them enough to bury them this tenderly. What they want now is to learn to forgive the world.

He leaves when the sun breaks its light over the dunes and the dunes secret the light away inside its grains. The sand blows around the metallic Tree, filling in the empty spaces, bracing it up straighter, taking the first bite from the base if it.

How Trees Came to Be
in the World

Before the Bang the entire Universe was smaller than an atom. The stars, the planets, all energy, all matter, all galaxies, were smaller than an atom. After the Bang, the Universe expanded like a bomb blast unfurling, and billions of years later, the Earth was formed from a cloud of dust and gas—the same stuff as the sun and stars. It was loud and hot and violent. Its core boiled, its surfaces exploded, meteorites and comets crashed into it and thick layers of dust blocked the light so that the planet was blanketed in darkness.

For millions of years it was like this, but when the dust settled, the unfiltered sunlight scorched the ground like a wildfire. There was no ozone and no ozone layer, no oxygen, only ammonia and hydrogen cyanide. Water could not settle on any surface; all the surfaces were too hot. All the land was rock, spewed from the mouths of volcanoes like streaming wads of chew.

The first life to emerge was a metabolizing slime that lived off of its own energy. They were naked slimes, without any coverings to protect them and vulnerable to whatever the world might bring. But in time, the most efficient of them drew together like a committee for community improvement. They developed membranes that allowed them to keep their genetic material close and the outside world out, so that when natural selection chose whom to favor, it passed over the naked and went with the protected.

These replicating slimes were the precursors of bacteria, archaea (bacteria like creatures), and the eukaryotic (modern) cells that make life as we know it possible. There is debate, of course, about which cells evolved first and how it all happened, but what is commonly believed is that these ancestral bacteria were simple, with their DNA looped and loosely corralled inside a cell wall, without a nucleus or organelles. They were primitive, adaptable, and strange. And they began to swallow things. It seems that they engulfed other bacteria and some archaea, too, and then the archaea began to engulf the bacteria back.

All of this engulfing was managed without mouths and without killing the other, and instead, the ingested creatures changed form and shifted function in order to survive on the inside. In fact, they not only shifted function, they created it. Some bacteria became mitochondria—the powerhouse of the cell—and some archaea turned into chloroplasts and colored the world green. They worked together to become complex cells with organelles and genetic information that was stored in more reliable ways, and so the modern eukaryotic cells came to be. How they imagined themselves into a thing that had previously not existed is a mystery, but there it is. The first single-celled organisms, tiny dots of algae, bobbed on the swamps of the world 3.8 billion years ago, and the more we know, the more we don't know. Faith is not the domain of religion alone.

These algae floated and spread and died and returned as if time were indiscriminate in its spending and all states of being were equally important and worth the years given to it. But the algae were made of adaptability - their mitochondria, their chloroplasts clicked and ticked and perfected their functioning through millions of generations of selection. And while they did this, the Earth stood empty and alone and covered in stone, and the seas broiled with the life that was evolving within. But eventually, and finally, like a late-blooming beauty, the algae hoisted itself onto land and sprouted bryophytes, which are the mosses and liverworts and hornworts.

These plants stayed small and flat and close to the water. Gravity pinned them to the ground and they couldn't grow upwards. When they tried to leave the wetlands dehydration took them by surprise and they shriveled and crisped and flaked. Time being abundant, they took plenty of it, but they did not overcome. The evolution of roots evaded them, leaves were an impossibility, more complex ways of transporting water never appeared. The bryophytes remained bryophytes and are bryophytes still.

So the algae tried again and hoisted more things onto the land. If even the Universe begins in miniature, everything else must, too. The first plants topped out at half an inch tall. They had not yet figured out how to grow roots, or leaves, or how to carry enough water from one part of themselves to the next, how to not let the sun scorch their tender green. And so, like the mosses, they sprouted close to the wetlands. They were spore-bound and completely dependent upon water to reproduce.

But the water was unreliable; it dried and flooded in turns. Newly evolved insects dragged their wingless bodies past the plants and through the ooze to the water when needed. But the plants could not drag, so they began to experiment. Until this point, their roots had only served as anchors against the winds, but soon, they sent out sprawling, hairlike growths over the surface of the hard rock. They shot strands upward beside their bodies and into the air, and they burst out sideways like frantic arms searching in the dark. But when they grew down into the rock they found secret pockets of water collected in pools and streams, and their roots evolved a use beyond anchoring. The plants pushed these roots into deeper and deeper places, mining for water until they were rich with it.

And then small cones of cells developed on the ends of the growing roots. They oozed mucus for protection as the tender shoots slid through the hard rock. These protective caps understood gravity below ground and told the roots to grow down and the plant to grow up. They traded glucose and sucrose with fungus for iron in return, and dug and thrived and dug and spread, until the Earth was acted upon by the things it had created. The roots forced their way through the rock in wild masses of plant life and spread and multiplied. They no longer only colonized the shores of the great oceans, they moved inland. They were an uncontainable force that drilled and crumbled the rock of the world. The roots pushed through and broke all things apart. Until in time, a very long time, there was soil.

It is difficult to imagine the silence then. There were still no birds diving over the waters, no lizards tossing out their tongues; nothing furred or scaled or skinned moved over the land—only ground bugs skittering on occasion, the wind, the tide's slapping, the Earth's occasional roar and stretch, rise and fall.

The planet floated in a soup of carbon dioxide and the tiny plants made the best of things and sucked it in deeply. They took it in through little slashes on their stems called stomata (rhymes with stigmata) because they still hadn't invented leaves. The chloroplasts in their cells nabbed the carbon and released the oxygen, and transformed the world again. The years are vast beyond imagining, but eventually, one little exhalation at a time, the plants pulled out vast quantities of carbon dioxide and replaced it with oxygen. They replaced it with so much oxygen that life evolved in consideration of it. There was even enough of it to feed the first wildfire that gobbled the first green like the slit-mouthed fish in the seas sucked at the seabed. But it didn't really matter to the plants, because the plants had taken over the land and they would only transform again.

To be a plant and to long for height, to desire more than half an inch distance from the ground requires the ability to raise one's limbs indefinitely. For a while, the plants depended on the water again. They sucked up large amounts of it and pumped their cells as full as they could, until they were plumped and tight and smooth like the skin of a drum, and in this way they were able to attain some height. But when the sun was hot and the water levels dropped, the plants did too. It was a disheartening way to live for a plant. So they invented lignin.

The creation of lignin changed everything. Plants coated their cells with it, and it made them strong; it made them able to grow tall enough to block out the sun, to provide roosts for birds and homes to the animals. They formed tunnels of lignin to transport water from the ground up, to the very tops of themselves, so that they could reach higher for the sun and higher into the world. With lignin, immensity became a possibility.

The first trees were like a sweetly naked Adam standing in the garden, smelling of dirt and formed from the stuff of the Earth. Like the first algae inspired plants, the trees were leafless with fronds like a fern and spores instead of seeds, but now they had roots and bark and wood and looked out over the ground from thirty feet above it. From these heights, 420 million years ago, it could have been seen that the ground was greening, the soil deepening, and the air turning.

The taller the trees grew, the more carbon dioxide they wanted, and the more carbon dioxide they wanted, the more they needed leaves. And so they invented them the way they invented all things—through trial and error and time. They gave them veins, created ways to keep them cool, told them to curl when the water was low and to drop away when the weather turned cold. And then there was one more sound in the world: the wind rising up through the branches and the rustling leaves within it.

The massive amounts of oxygen released from the trees swaddled the Earth like a protective membrane, and the ozone grew and the sunlight softened. The carbon was sucked from the air, stored inside the trees and buried safely in the ground with every fallen trunk. The trees were pressed and pressured for millions of years into the great oil pools of the Earth, and the carbon that they stored is what is rereleased back into the air when that oil is burned like a race to return to the prelife world.

The continents drifted as the Universe drifted. The waters receded and more dry land appeared, and what was left were lakes and ponds and puddles where once was sea. Stranded fish that had evolved and thrived for millions of years rotted in the sun, their gills opened and closed in vain until the end.

Three hundred sixty million years ago, the shade of the trees dappled the beaches like clouds over the waves and small insects moved below the branches. The remaining fish became hungry. They roamed through the murky waters hunting food that no longer existed. They grew strange and deformed and lifted their heads above the shrinking waters to see what was beyond them. Then, there might have been a first gasp in the world before the first creature threw itself out of the pond and onto dry land, slapping its awkward limbs toward the food beneath the trees.

And there was evening and there was morning that day for the creature.

Living in the Trees

FOR TWO YEARS I LIVED in the trees with my daughter in
my mother's basement, in a suburb called Sherwood Park on
Alder Avenue in Alberta. Birch Avenue was down the road, and
Fir Street a few blocks over; it was a forest of names. We lived
in a cold little cave underground, where we slept with roots and
worms at face level just beyond the concrete wall. It was the
time in my life when I was sick and newly divorced, when my
house had burned down and my dad was smoking crack.

Upstairs, in the warmer months, the leaves clicked
against one other in the wind like a momma clucking comfort
to her baby, but in the winter, Alberta became an arid desert
of snow. I woke in the mornings with bloody knuckles and a
cracked lip as if I had been fighting all night long. I'd stumble
out of bed to make coffee with water from the bathroom sink

downstairs, measuring the scoops in the dark with my fingers like a blind woman.

One winter, the temperature dropped to minus forty and hovered there for days. We waited it out in the basement for a while, our pale soft bodies growing paler and softer like blind bugs under stones, and when it became too much, we tried to leave, but the car door wouldn't shut in the cold. We sat for a moment on the frozen seats and then shuffled back through the drifts and down the stairs in our heavy coats and boots and watched the window wells fill to the top with snow until there was no daylight at all. We colored, we read, we painted, we slept.

Eventually, the thermometer climbed its skinny red ladder a rung or two, and reading in bed late one night, I threw off the quilts, put on all my warmest clothes and went out for a walk.

Just past our house was a large open field with a graveyard edged by copses of frozen poplars, and I walked toward it. The kind of poplars that grow in Alberta are mostly aspens, and an aspen is an iceberg; its real glory is below ground and only known by the buried and the things that eat the buried. Aspens live in clonal colonies, and what looks like many trees growing together is really only one. Sprouted suckers shoot for acres from the same enormous root. The heaviest living thing in the world is an aspen, and the oldest. There's one in Utah that's been sending out suckers for 80,000 years. In ancient times, aspens were called the Tree That Transcends Fear and shields were made of its wood. They were thought to attract money and bring hope, and their buds, when gathered into a tiny red bag and placed under a pillow, healed a broken heart.

The graveyard I walked through to get to the trees was one of those modern kinds—fearless, tidied, organized against any real acknowledgment of death. People "passed" here, they did not die. I walked past the Christians tucked away under their corner of land, then the Taoists in theirs, and the Muslims in another. The little stream beside the Chinese pagoda was frozen and so full of snow I could hardly tell where it would be come spring. Some guard dogs barked at me from a distance.

There were burnt bits of fake Chinese money scattered in the snow, and one grave was heaped with mounds of frozen flowers wrapped in plastic, some with the netting still around the buds to protect them in the shipping. The pile reached as high as my waist. I twisted off a single yellow rose to keep warm in my coat, and in its place I put a fuzzy cattail that I had picked on the walk. It was so dry that the light wind sent the seeds up and out into the space beyond the fence.

Poplars belong to the dead. Hades' lover was transformed into a white one upon her death, and Herakles wore a wreath of the leaves on his head when he emerged from the Underworld—but there were none inside this graveyard. I climbed over the barbed-wire fence, took a shortcut through a field and headed for the aspen grove.

The snow was up to my knees, and my ankles, where the pants had been pushed up as I plowed through the drifts, were numb. My scarf was stuck to my face and my lashes grew ice as I walked. I paused on the top of a small bald hill where I could look out over the distance and see the path back to my house in the moonlight. It seemed so far away. It would be nice, I thought, to just lie in the snow for a while without moving, to wait, to have someone scoop me up and carry me like a baby from a car to a warm bed. So I sat on my knees, deciding, and watched the empty fields.

When I went down into the valley from the hill and entered the trees, I noticed at the edge something small and bright flickering in the unmarked snow. I walked towards it and kicked at the thing by my feet. It was a plastic St. Nicholas, the patron saint of generosity, lying face down in his red velvet cloak.

I picked him up and settled him in the branches of an aspen, and he looked down on me from his perch, one arm lifted over me in a blessing. I turned to leave for a moment and then stopped, faced him, and stepped forward to let his open hand rest over my head.

Before I left, I held out my hand over him in return. I blessed the plastic, the saint, the ground, the poplars, their buried selves. I said the words as if they could stick, as if goodness could be stored inside of these things like a cup for anyone else that might pass by. When I was done, I turned and pocketed a five-dollar bill half-buried in the snow and walked back to my house in the trees.

Cardinal

ONE DARK MORNING AFTER his resurrection and just before Jesus flew up into heaven, he came to my backyard in the form of a cardinal and balanced on the telephone wire with his skinny black legs. It was early spring, before anything had bloomed, and the grass was gray and mush and rotted. Jesus stood in the sky and whistled the whistle all cardinals do, which sounds something like, "Pretty girl, pretty girl."

The sun rose as red as the feathers on his cardinal back and pushed the night off the edge of the world. I saw that it was time for Jesus to return to God, but that he did not want to leave his wire. "Pretty girl, pretty girl, pretty girl," he cried out over the vast and winding Earth.

Thanks

I would like to express my gratitude to the Nonfiction Writing program at the University of Iowa, to my peers and teachers there, and specifically to John D'Agata for his generosity of time and investment in my work.

Thanks as well to my mini-workshop group—for rolling your eyes at my overly sentimental messes and underlining the good bits. I adore you, Inara Verzemnieks, Ariel Lewiton, Mary Helen Kennerly, Lucas Mann, Lina Maria Ferreira Cabeza Vanegas, Kristen Radtke.

Thanks to Sarabande Books and Sarah Gorham for taking me on and guiding me along with patience and kindness, and to Kristen Radtke for your hard work, openness and for my beautiful cover design.

Thank you, Danielle Degen and Melanie Stork for remaining my oldest and dearest.

I am, of course, also thankful to my siblings and parents—Caroline and Jeff Dux, Chris and Nadine Davies, Kim and Remi De Champlain, Tammy McMillan, Brian Davies, Courtney Moberly, Herb and Jackie Wiebe, Glen Davies, and Roger and Sherri Stewart for all of your support and encouragement and help. I am especially grateful to my mother, Catharina Pelster Davies who has always loved me in ways both practical and inspirational.

Thank you, dear India Sophia Stewart Pelster-Wiebe. Daughters do not come more delightful or lovely or wonderful than you.

And thank you, dear Richard. Let's live long together, so that I can show you the extent of my gratitude and love.

Angela Pelster has an MFA from the University of Iowa's Nonfiction Writing program and her essays have appeared in *Granta, The Gettysburg Review, Seneca Review, The Globe and Mail, Relief Magazine,* and others. Her children's novel *The Curious Adventures of India Sophia* won the Golden Eagle Children's Choice award in 2006. She lives with her family in Baltimore and teaches at Towson University.

Sarabande Books thanks you for the purchase of this book; we do hope you enjoy it! Founded in 1994 as an independent, nonprofit, literary press, Sarabande publishes poetry, short fiction, and literary nonfiction—genres increasingly neglected by commercial publishers. We are committed to producing beautiful, lasting editions that honor exceptional writing, and to keeping those books in print. If you're interested in further reading, take a moment to browse our website at sarabandebooks.org. There you'll find information about other titles; opportunities to contribute to the Sarabande mission; and an abundance of supporting materials including audio, video, a lively blog, and our Sarabande in Education program.